For Jack and Dan – without them, it wouldn't have been possible.

FOUR SUNS
PRODUCTIONS

© Paul Kendall, 2023

PLEASE ALLOW ME TO INTRODUCE MYSELF...

On a balmy spring evening, in April 2013, I was sitting in the garden of our Hertfordshire home. I had a cold beer in my hand and was looking out on a clear twilight sky, framed by trees just coming into full leaf. I was being serenaded by birdsong and the occasional distant rumble of jets flying in or out of Heathrow airport. But my mood was nowhere near as tranquil as my surroundings.

I'd just had the latest in a long and frustrating succession of email exchanges with the people who control Bob Dylan's song publishing in the UK. We wanted to use two of the great man's songs in a documentary we were making, about the former Byrd and pioneering singer/songwriter, Gene Clark.

One was The Byrds' ground-breaking version of 'Mr Tambourine Man', which had propelled the band to worldwide stardom in 1965 and given Gene an early commercial peak. The other was a ramshackle but heartfelt reading of 'I Shall Be Released', performed by Gene and a bunch of mates sitting round his kitchen table, on a previously unseen home movie clip.

The former would be central to the chapter of the film about The Byrds and Gene's short lived but game-changing involvement with them. The latter had been earmarked, from the very beginning, as the conclusion to the film, both actual and emotional.

Dylan's publishers, however, were unmoved by our pleas that we were embarked on a low budget labour of love, about a fellow musician who their client much admired. They were adamant in demanding license fees that were way above what we had painstakingly negotiated with the owners of all the other songs we were planning to use. Nearly forty titles, in total. The argument we had successfully employed with the publishers of Gene's own songs – that we would be drawing attention to an artist who had been largely forgotten – unsurprisingly carried absolutely no weight with Bob's representatives. Who, seemingly, had never heard of Gene Clark.

To make matters even worse, accepting their demands would trigger the 'most favoured nations' clause in everyone else's contracts. A phrase we were unfamiliar with, before starting this project, but which would hang over it like a vulture ready to swoop on an unwary victim. Essentially it meant that if any one of the companies got a better deal, all the others would then be entitled to enjoy the same terms. The cost of music licensing, which was already by far the most expensive part of producing the film, would instantly become completely unaffordable.

As I sipped my beer, without really tasting it, it seemed we had two options. Not use the two Dylan songs, which would seriously diminish the film. Or simply abandon it, throwing away two years of work and a substantial chunk of my pension fund, which had already been spent. (It was a dilemma that other film makers had faced before us and continue to face. There are several music documentaries, sitting unseen on the shelf or no longer available, which have foundered on that same reef of unsympathetic or unco-operative rights owners.)

If you've seen the film, you'll know that we didn't take option one. And, as you're reading this book, you'll have guessed that option two also didn't apply. So how did we get over the substantial hurdle that Mr Dylan had inadvertently put in our way? And how did a father and two young sons manage to put together a film that would be praised around the world and screened several times by the BBC, with an almost complete lack of the resources and experience usually associated with serious film making? You'll have to read on.

Hopefully, by the end, you'll be thinking "If they can do it, why can't I?". There are stories waiting to be told and the appropriate technology is now within pretty much everyone's reach. So if you have the ideas and the belief and the determination, you have no real excuse for not diving in and doing it. I hope you find it as fulfilling as I have.

IN THE BEGINNING

Where did the journey to making a film about Gene Clark begin? Was it when I first heard a Dillard & Clark song on the radio and became aware of his name? When he was one of the last people I interviewed, during my time as a music journalist in the mid '70s? Or when I got his biography as a Christmas present in 2010?

I think it was much earlier than that. Producing the film could be seen as the culmination of a process whereby music became a central part of my life and which led up to my feeling able to commit – feeling compelled to commit, even – to a project that would be so demanding, in so many ways.

That process started with me as a toddler, perched on either the draining board or the kitchen table next to my mother while she did the housework, listening to classical music on The Third Programme – BBC Radio's 'highbrow' station, which was the forerunner of today's Radio 3.

Then came 'Children's Favourites' on The Light Programme (the 'low brow' station, now Radio 2), hosted by a man calling himself Uncle Mac and playing the likes of 'Old MacDonald Had A Farm' and 'The Teddy Bears Picnic'. It was later suggested that Uncle Mac's interest in his young audience extended beyond entertaining them, but he was only in touch with me over the airwaves.

Things started to get more serious when I was about ten years old and became a devotee of 'Pick Of The Pops', the Sunday afternoon unveiling of the latest Top Ten and one of the BBC's very few concessions to pop music, prior to the launch of Radio 1 a few years later. I can still remember the actual physical tremor of excitement that ran through me, when I first heard 'I Wanna Hold Your Hand' as it zoomed up the charts in November 1963.

It can't have been too much later that my musical path took a significant turn. One of my cousins, who was several years older than me, was a big music fan. I'd stay with his family for a few days each year and, while I was there, he'd play me the stuff that he favoured. As they lived within reach of the specialist record shops of Central London, he was able to buy records that would have been unobtainable almost anywhere else in the country and, with hindsight, he had excellent taste.

As soon as I was exposed to the likes of John Lee Hooker, Muddy Waters and Howlin' Wolf, I could appreciate that this was something completely different to the ephemeral fluff that made up the bulk of the British hit parade in the early '60s. It was music produced by men, not boys, with a depth and passion that I hadn't encountered before. It was a little unnerving at first, but I came to love it and almost anything else seemed lightweight by comparison.

Music created on my side of the Atlantic soon grew up, however, as a host of great bands – The Stones, The Kinks, The Animals, The Who, The Small Faces, etc etc – followed in the footsteps of the Fab Four. But the next real landmark in my musical awakening came in the summer of 1965 and it involved yet another American icon.

My family – or, to be more precise, my mother – had decided that our annual family holiday would be taken in the company of some sort of Christian Fellowship group, gathering at Doddington Hall, an 18th century country pile in Cheshire. The mornings were taken up with prayer meetings or discussion groups or whatever, for the adults, while the kids were escorted off to the swimming baths in the nearest town. Unfortunately, or maybe fortunately, I'd acquired some verrucas on my feet from the changing rooms at the school gym, which meant I wasn't allowed to join them. For several hours each day, I was left to amuse myself as best I could.

Doddington Hall was huge and set in extensive parkland, so there was plenty to explore. It was a girls' boarding school, at the time, and one of my earliest discoveries was a games room in the basement of the main house. The centrepiece of the room was two table tennis tables, which were put to good use in the afternoons and evenings, when I had someone to play with. The other thing that caught my eye was a reel-to-reel tape recorder, tucked away in a corner. I'd never seen such a thing before and it took me a while to work out how to operate it, before I could play the one tape that was available.

That tape was labelled 'Bob Dylan – Bringing It All Back Home'. The name meant nothing to me. 'Blowin' In The Wind' had been a big hit for Peter, Paul & Mary two years earlier, and The Byrds' genre defining version of 'Mr Tambourine Man' was one of the sounds of that summer, but I had no idea who they were written by or that they were the work of the same person.

What came out of the machine within those venerable walls was revelatory. The raw voice had echoes of the bluesmen that I was already familiar with, while the rockier songs, which made up half the album, were in similar musical territory to what was being ventured into by British R&B bands at the time. But the lyrics were like nothing I'd heard before – complex, poetic, allusive and apparently espousing a world view that challenged almost everything that a well behaved, middle class English boy had been brought up to accept as the norm. It would be a couple more years before I became familiar with Aldous Huxley and Jim Morrison, but the bloody doors of perception were blown off right there. I listened to the album at least once every day of the holiday, absorbing it to the point where I could recite most of the words by heart.

I think I can identify that as the moment when music took over from cricket as my great passion, and my dreams of emulating my boyhood hero, Fred Trueman, and playing for England, were forgotten. Music was no longer merely an entertainment but a guide to being, and I became set on making it what I did for a living. Either performing it or writing about it or working in the music business.

I started learning to play the guitar (I'm still learning, more than half a century later) and voraciously hunted down new musical experiences and new voices, through radio, TV and friends. Official radio in the UK – which basically meant the BBC – was a pretty useless source, before Radio 1 was launched in September 1967, and TV wasn't much better. 'Top Of The Pops' was a weekly opportunity to see chart acts in the flesh, while the much loved 'Ready Steady Go' gave fabulous introductions to artists as diverse as Jimi Hendrix and Jim Reeves, until it was inexplicably cancelled at the end of 1966. That was more or less it, though. Much better were Radio Luxembourg and the pirate stations – especially Radio Caroline and Radio London – which allowed DJs such as Johnnie Walker and Kenny Everett a free hand to play a wide range of music, old and new. Particularly influential was John Peel, whose shows on Radio London were essential listening and a gateway to the latest sounds from the States and on home soil.

By the time I was in the sixth form at school, the common room was another forum for musical exchange and my preferences had started to solidify around the holy trinity of blues, folk and country, and blends thereof. Which put me at odds with some of my peers, many of whom favoured the self-indulgent noodlings of bands such as Cream and Ten Years After, and who often gained possession of the common room record player through force of numbers. More satisfactory were the break time listening sessions organised by one of the chemistry teachers, who took great delight in opening young ears to the esoteric likes of Captain Beefheart and The Incredible String Band. He was also responsible for organising an excursion to my first ever proper gig – Pink Floyd at the Royal Albert Hall, no less.

Once bitten by the live music bug, there was no stopping me. I was blessed to be growing up in Aylesbury, an otherwise unremarkable

Buckinghamshire market town that was home to a fantastic music club called Friars. Over the next few years I was able to see a whole host of legends at close quarters: David Bowie (pre- and post-Ziggy Stardust), Mott The Hoople, Roxy Music, The MC5, Lou Reed, Iggy Pop... while the list isn't endless, it's certainly very long and pretty impressive, and can be found in its entirety on the Friars Aylesbury website. And when I went to college in 1971, the repertoire of convenient live music options was extended by Oxford Polytechnic – another intimate venue where I witnessed Richard & Linda Thompson, Eagles (the original line-up, not the multi-platinum selling bunch), Jeff Beck and Beefheart with The Magic Band, to name but a few. Both places benefitted from being within an hour of London but quite separate from it, so bands who would usually be playing much bigger venues were happy to visit them as warm-up gigs for tours or as PR showcases.

When I finished college in 1974, I came back to Aylesbury. A hometown sweetheart was waiting for me, a pair of musician friends were getting a first taste of success and, as well as boasting the illustrious music club, it was also the base for a small but well-respected magazine called *Zigzag*. *Zigzag* was run by a guy called Pete Frame and was literally a cottage industry, put together on the floor of his thatched abode in a nearby village, which usually reeked intoxicatingly of cow gum. Pete is best known for his Rock Family Trees, which are miracles of research, draughtsmanship and calligraphy (available in book form from all good sellers). But he's also a great writer and turned out to be an invaluable mentor, welcoming me into the *Zigzag* family and giving me opportunities to meet and write about many of my heroes and heroines.

For the next four years I was caught up in a heady maelstrom of music-related activities and my dreams of a life somehow revolving around music looked to be coming true. My two musical friends formed a band, in which I was the bass player; I got involved with running the Friars club and the record store that was linked to it; and I became a regular writer for *Zigzag*, which led on to work with other publications. If I wasn't playing gigs with the band, I was helping to organise them or going to review them. The relationship with my hometown sweetheart also blossomed. We got married in 1978 and are together to this day.

Things changed, however, as they are wont to do. And not necessarily for the better. As my writing career expanded and the band got busier, I had to give up working with Friars. Then the writing started to lose its appeal. I'd set out with the intention of just covering people who I liked and sharing my enthusiasm for them. My first ever interviewee was Emmylou Harris, on her maiden voyage to the UK. She seemed to be as nervous as I was and made my baptism painless by chattering non-stop for an hour, in response to my first question, unwittingly answering nearly all the others in the process. The likes of Jackson Browne, JJ Cale, Carlos Santana, Lowell George and Lou Reed followed, and *Zigzag* gave me the space and freedom to write about them as I saw fit. But other publications were more prescriptive and, to generate a living income, I found myself accepting commissions involving artists for whom I struggled to summon much interest. The low point came when I spent an afternoon listening to the members of America (who I considered to be second rate Neil Young impersonators) bemoan their declining success, and I decided there and then that I no longer wished to be a music journalist.

One of my final commissions took me to meeting Gene Clark. A fateful encounter, although I didn't realise it at the time. He'd come over to the UK with his band of the moment, as part of a kind of package tour with Roger McGuinn and Chris Hillman – two of the other original Byrds – and their bands. Each did their own set and then the three of them came together for an extended encore of Byrds songs. I saw the show at the Hammersmith Odeon (now the Hammersmith Apollo), then went north with the tour party to see further shows in Leeds and Liverpool, giving me an opportunity to speak with Gene at some point along the way.

The interview in the Liverpool hotel bar was supposed to end after the regulation one hour, but the evening's gig got cancelled – I found out later that the tour was fraught with financial difficulties and eventually got cut short, leaving Gene and his band stranded with no funds for flying home. So after I turned off my tape machine we just carried on talking over a few beers. Gene impressed me as a very un-starlike star, humble and quite vulnerable. I particularly remember that, as we chatted, he genuinely seemed to be as interested in me and my thoughts as I was in him. Not the usual arrangement between a rookie scribe and a seasoned performer/interviewee.

Clearly I got lucky. While we were making the film about him I was regaled with stories of his wild and self-destructive behaviour when under the influence. And there's a chapter in Allan Jones's hugely entertaining 'Can't Stand Up For Falling Down' book, recounting his attempts to interview Gene for *Melody Maker* during the same tour, which tells a very different story. "I meet Gene Clark in a record company office", Allan writes, "At least that's where I am. Where Gene is, I couldn't possibly say".

Before we go any further, here's the piece I wrote for *Zigzag* after interviewing Gene:

On the one hand, a poet - prophet, seer or sage, call him what you will (he'd much prefer not to be called any of those things) - and on the other, a pioneer in what, for lack of a more precise terminology, we will refer to as country rock. Like the title of his last album suggests, there are two sides to Gene Clark's story...at least.

But where does the story begin? With his epochal 'No Other' album, the ultimate fusion of those aforementioned elements; or with 'White Light' three years earlier, where they were first really starting to come together? With the short-lived Dillard & Clark Expedition (whose name emphasises the forays they were making into uncharted territory); or with The Byrds, who took Gene too near the sun too soon, forcing him back to earth to reassess himself and his art? Maybe with The New Christy Minstrels, or the Kansas City folk scene where they found the 21 year old Clark in 1962? Or maybe even back in his Missouri childhood, with the dual influences of a multi-instrumentalist, country music loving father and the new excitement of rock'n'roll?

For Gene himself, however, the story goes back much further than that...both for himself and Thomas Jefferson Kaye, the veteran producer who first worked with Gene on 'No Other' and stayed on to produce 'Two Sides To Every Story', join Gene's band, and become what can only be described as a soul brother.

"Tommy and I write almost everything together now", he explains, "because our communication is excellent and we're able to exchange thoughts well, both musically and lyrically. I would even venture that Tommy and I have probably been partners for many lifetimes, and you could say that we are cosmically or psychically connected. We know and feel what we're doing instinctively, and to say how that comes about, my best thought of it is that the universe being a function of rotations from the atom or molecule right on out to wherever the end of the universe is, so everything runs in cycles...and to say that we only live one lifetime, or that the only civilisation is right here on this earth, is ludicrous".

Describing himself as "not religious, but spiritual in my attitude towards life", Gene feels that this outlook shows through in all his work, but it's most apparent on 'No Other', which was recorded during the first half of 1974, after a lengthy period of preparation.

"Most of my writing comes from a spiritual place. I think that true art forms in poetry and music, or the joining together of poetry and music, come from a spiritual place. Any amount of soul-searching, whether it be by a novelist, or a film maker, or anyone, makes for a more profound statement.

"For example, the 'No Other' album was written when I had a house overlooking the Pacific Ocean in North-

The first of the cosmic cowboys continues to ride the range, accompanied by his trusty sidekick Thomas Jefferson Kaye.

GENE CLARK

BOTH SIDES UP

Tom Cheyenne

JUNE 1977 ZIGZAG

ern California. I would just sit in the living room, which had a huge bay window, and stare at the ocean for hours at a time. People would come in and say 'How come you're not doing anything...how can you just sit here?'. But I would have a pen and paper there, and a guitar or piano, and pretty soon a thought would come, and I'd write it down or put it on tape. In many instances with the 'No Other' album, after a day of meditation looking at something which is a very natural force, I'd come up with something.

"I feel that any pure force is based on the rhythm of universal motion, and anything operated on that natural force is much more spiritual. It isn't contrived...or if it is we don't know about it, and it was done by a much higher mind than we know about. So I feel that tuning into a more natural force, or higher element, can maybe inspire you to come up with a more factual statement...or a more spiritual statement.

"Going back to that thing about cycles in lifetimes...somehow I knew of these things even as a small child, but I didn't know how to express them or sort them out. Through my experience of meeting people who I felt were higher minds and influences, and observing their way of expressing feelings, I've found that I've grown in my self-expression... although I don't claim to have the cat by the tail, I'm still a novice".

The years between Harold Eugene Clark's birth (or reincarnation) and the release of 'No Other' in September '74 have been fully documented in ZZ49, so we take up the story (from all sides) in February 1972 when Gene, after abortive attempts to record a successor to 'White Light' for A&M, signed with Asylum.

As things turned out, however, his first work for Asylum was not as a solo artist, but as part of the oft-rumoured and finally accomplished Byrds reunion.

"That album had been discussed for ages, and finally I got a call from David Crosby one night, and he suggested we just got together to see how it worked, and that's really all there was to it. We could have done it a lot better if we'd taken more time and rehearsed it longer. If we had sorted out arrangements and material for six months and not tried to produce it ourselves, we could have had a great album, rather than an OK album".

Especially in comparison with the overall lameness of the record, Gene came out of the project with his dignity reasonably well preserved, in fact. His 'Full Circle', left over from the final A&M sessions, was very apt as a kind of theme song for the reunion and pleasant enough, and 'Changing Heart' was probably the strongest song written for the album, although neither really gave any clue of the greatness that was shortly to follow.

In the months after the Byrds album, Gene spent most of his time in the seclusion of Northern California, breaking off from his intensive songwriting period only to do a few gigs with The Adventures of Roger McGuinn during the summer of '73.

Meanwhile, back in LA, Thomas Jefferson Kaye was embroiled in the recording of Bobby Neuwirth's solo album for Asylum, which was already running $140,000 over budget, despite the fact that Neuwirth's many, many friends were all supplying their services free of charge.

"At one session", says Kaye, "Neuwirth and Dylan were sitting there, and we were talking about songwriters, and they both said that their three favourite songwriters in the world were Bob Dylan, Bobby Charles and Gene Clark. Then three days later, David Geffen called me, feeling - I think - that the only way to get me to finish the Bobby Neuwirth record was to offer me another project, and he asked whether I wanted to produce Gene Clark or Jackson Browne...and I said Gene Clark. He said 'That's interesting', but didn't ask me why. The reason is simply that I prefer Gene Clark. They're both great artists, but I felt I could do more with Gene, because he's always different".

Kaye is a fascinating character, worthy of several Zigzag pages in his own right. Raised on a reservation in North Dakota, he somehow ended up in New York City at the age of seventeen, producing smash hits for The Shirelles, and within two years he was head of A&R at Scepter Records, earning $300,000 a year and turning out more hits, like 'Killer Joe' by The Rocky Fellers. Since then he's had his name attached to innumerable sessions, as well as making two very under-rated solo albums for ABC. A man who's seen it all and done it all...and kept coming back for more. I just wish we had space to pass on a few of the outrageous and hilarious stories he has to tell.

Undaunted by the lavish expense of the Neuwirth album, he and Clark managed to run up another enormous bill in the recording of 'No Other', spending several months recording in LA and mixing in San Francisco, using a large cast of the West Coast's finest.

It was well worth it, though. The songs that Gene brought down from Mendocino are just magnificent - gorgeous swirling melodies and provoking, emotive (if often enigmatic) lyrics - and the standard of playing on the album is absolutely inspired. Between them all - and Gene and Tommy give especial credit to keyboard player Michael Utley, who apparently had a large hand in the arrangements - they came up with a record which defies musical categorisation, blending rock, pop, country, gospel and soul into a brilliantly unique whole, and which has something to say to anyone with the ears to listen.

"I was strongly influenced at that time by two other artists", Gene recalls. "Stevie Wonder's 'Innervisions' album and 'Goat's Head Soup'. When I was writing 'No Other' I concentrated on those albums a lot, and was very inspired by the direction of them...which is ironic, because 'Innervisions' is a very climbing, spiritual thing, while 'Goat's Head Soup' has connotations of the lower forces as well. But somehow the joining of the two gave me a place to go with 'No Other', and I wanted it to go in a powerful direction".

In keeping with the seriousness of the songs, and in contrast with the mayhem that Kaye had to contend with on the Neuwirth sessions, 'No Other' was recorded in a very disciplined manner. Except for one night when Sly Stone apparently marched into the studio with a whole stream of flunkeys carrying tables and chairs and a full-scale banquet, it was business first all the way - even Gene and Tommy's ex-wives were unceremoniously ejected from the studio on one occasion - and the musicians were extended to the full.

"We had some really incredible musicians involved on the album: Michael Utley and Jerry McGee from The Dixie Flyers, Butch Trucks, Joe Lala, Lee Sklar and lots of other really high echelon musicians. But it was really hard to record, because the concept and approach that Tommy and I were taking was fairly foreign to them, and it took them a lot of time in the studio before we could actually get the songs to the point we wanted them.

"In fact, the track 'No Other' was cut for one solid week before we decided we'd got a take. So it was like pulling teeth in one respect, because everybody was used to doing things by a completely different method. But once they got it, of course, they were alright. It wasn't hard to get on tape, it was just hard to perform it at first".

By the way, if you ever wondered how they got that strange, otherworldly vocal sound on the title track, it was done by double-tracking Gene's vocal and recording the second layer over one of the studio telephones. Tommy reckons that "As a producer, that's my answer to Brian Wilson...I don't listen to it too much anymore, because if I did I'd always be trying to outdo it".

Unfortunately, at the time of release 'No Other' got more or less lost in the shuffle with Asylum's more commercially heavyweight acts, and only now are its many merits being widely recognised.

"I was really disappointed that 'No Other' wasn't more successful", Gene admits. "Of course, now it's getting more attention than it ever did, and has been reissued, but I think it was misunderstood generally by the public and the media".

From the way Tommy tells it, in fact, one of the people who failed to appreciate the album initially was David Geffen himself.

"I brought 'No Other' into David's

Tom Cheyenne

BOTH SIDES UP

office to play it for him, and I was
so proud. David took the record out
of the sleeve and counted the bands,
and he looked at me, and said "There
are only eight songs on this record?
It cost $92,000 to make!!"...and he
just threw the record down on his
desk. There were more songs, but
Gene didn't want to edit what we'd
got, and we didn't have the budget
for a double album, and anyway, we
felt it made the statement he wanted
to make".

With the release of 'N
Other' in September of
'74, Gene went on the
road with a backing
band called The Silver-
ados, doing mostly
small college and club gigs, and in
his time off started doing demos of
the songs he'd been writing for his
next album. Tommy takes up the story:
"Gene made a demo of five or six
songs so that Asylum could hear what
he was going to do for his next record. He did 'Sister Moon', 'Home
Run King', 'Hear The Wind', 'Kansas
City Southern' and 'Lonely Saturday', and when they heard them at
Asylum, they told Gene that they
didn't hear anything. In fact they
thought it was terrible, and that's
when they gave him his release".

Rather than look for another deal
right away, Gene and Tommy started
recording on their own account, and
waited until it was almost finished
before offering it to interested
parties.

"A lot of companies passed on this
album, but Al Coury (A&R chief at
RSO in America) on the first listen
said 'OK, that's it'...we only played him rough mixes, but he under-

stood exactly what we were doing.
The reason it took a long time to
make the deal was that we were also
negotiating with CBS and RCA, and
don't like to go around playing
everybody off against each other.
"Asylum also called us and said
that although they didn't have Gene
anymore, they'd really love to hear
what he was doing, so we sent them
over the album, and they said "Hey,
what are you guys trying to do, pull
a fast one? That's the same demo
that we paid for!"...oh boy, am I
glad we're out of there! So it took
about nine months...this record was
really due to come out around last
August, but when we made the deal
there were problems with the cover,
and then Clapton and The Bee Gees
had releases scheduled, and Al Coury
wanted to wait on us until 1977".

In comparison with the ecstatic
musical richness and lyrical depth
of 'No Other', 'Two Sides To Every
Story' was a disappointment for many
people (myself included).

Partly, one would imagine, because
of budget restrictions, and partly
because of their different attitude
to the record, it's a far looser,
more spontaneous album, with several
glimpses of Gene's earthier musical
heritage as well as his more cosmic
preoccupations. The re-recording of
'Kansas City Southern', he admits
himself, was done as a kind of clue
to his intentions, and the feel of
the album - is of a deliberate attempt to portray both sides of Gene's
artistic character.

"That's a really good analogy", he
agreed when I made that suggestion
to him, "because 'No Other' was so
misunderstood by so many people that
I felt maybe if I could start bringing the two influences together,
eventually they would grow to a
point where in an album or two's
time, it would be even further out
than 'No Other' musically. To where
the earthiness and grittiness of the

rock feeling would be there, along
with the more ethereal, mystical
(as I've been told) effect of 'No
Other'".

Although the record has several
real high points, especially the
graceful 'Sister Moon' and the
wistful 'Past Addresses', the inclusion of old chestnuts like 'Marylou'
and Gene's own 'Kansas City Southern' really rock the boat so far as
the mood of the album as a whole is
concerned, and the sense of vision
and purpose that contributed so
largely to the aesthetic success of
'No Other' seems to be sadly lacking. Gene, however, would certainly
disagree:

"I purposely did the album that
way, because I wanted to give a
little commercial value to it, so
that more people might pay attention
to it. Not everyone in the public
has the references or the consciousness to be able to understand a very
profound and artistic statement.
It's like saying that everyone should
have a Picasso on their wall...not
everyone can look at a Picasso and
get anything out of it, but put them
in a situation where he's sketched
something more commercial as well as
very artistic, and people are bound
to see it better, and it leads them
into the higher forms of the man's
art too.

"I feel that holds true in The
Byrds electric folk-rock version of
'Mr.Tambourine Man', which brought
a loy more people into a Bob Dylan
consciousness, whereas before they
had thought of Dylan as the guy
with the weird voice, and never
really gotten into the depths of
what he was delivering".

So...it looks like we can stand
and whistle for something compar-
able to 'No Other' until Gene's got
the gold albums he seems to be
after. Personally, I think he's making a big mistake. He's most unlikely ever to emulate The Eagles or

Fleetwood Mac in terms of sales, no matter what he does, but at least work of the quality of 'White Light' and 'No Other' would guarantee him a devoted and increasingly large following, whereas the direction of 'Two Sides' looks likely to end up falling awkwardly between two stools. But no doubt time will show the wiser, and with the news that the album appears to be crossing over into the country charts in the States, it could be that he and Tommy will be proved right in their judgement... commercial acceptability still seems a pretty bogus priority when you're making music, though.

Once the recording of 'Two Sides' was completed, Gene started to think about getting a new band together to go on the road after its release, The Silverados having been disbanded some months earlier after almost two years together.

The guys he originally chose were Billy Shay on guitar, bassist Peter Oliva and drummer Andy Kandanes, along with a keyboard player and extra percussionist.

"Peter, Andy and Billy basically grew up together and played together in different groups off and on, and we've all been the best of friends for five or six years. We'd jam occasionally, and get together to play records, or have dinner, or talk about it all, but we'd never really played as a group because we'd al-

ways been involved in something else".

Hardly had they started rehearsals up at Gene's Mendocino ranch, when Tommy Kaye came up to visit Gene for the weekend, and stayed right up till now!

"Tommy heard the group and ended up renting a house, joining the band, and he and I started writing a whole bunch of tunes and re-arranging old songs and so forth, and after the third rehearsal we knew that we really had something going. We rehearsed about five hours a day, six days a week, and it got to be really a daily pleasure that we looked forward to...we had a sound system set up in the living room of the house that's on the album cover. After a time the conga player and keyboard player didn't gell musically with the direction that the rest of us were heading in, so they left".

It's probably unfair to judge the Kansas City Southern Band (K for Kaye and C for Clark, geddit... there's two sides to every band name too, it seems) on the evidence of their curtailed British tour, where they were only getting the chance to play about 40 minutes of the two hour set that they've got prepared, but they seem to be carrying on the drive for greater commercial acceptance that was begun with 'Two Sides To Every Story'. They put the emphasis on rocking out, and very entertaining it is too, especially at

the Leeds gig where they came on cold without a soundcheck and really pulled it out of the bag. It's definitely music for the body rather than the soul, though.

Plans for the future include an album using the KC Southern Band, who apparently acquitted themselves very well in the studio when they recorded some publishing demos recently; another solo album for Tommy, again using Gary Katz as the producer; and - hold onto your hats! - a Dillard & Clark Expedition reunion!

"Right...one of the things we've been toying around with is getting the entire cast of Dillard & Clark back together again. Bernie Leadon, who's been making a brand new album up at his house with Glyn Johns, is seriously interested, and we'd like to get Donna Washburn and Byron Berline and David Jackson, who's just left The Alpha Band and is now playing with Cher. David's like that... he has to play everything, and I respect that. He'd play with Lawrence Welk just to find out what it was like.

"We'll probably just get together with a bunch of songs and take it wherever it is today. It'll probably be an extension of the 'Don't Let Me Down' cut from 'Through The Morning Through The Night'. We probably wouldn't tour, just do an album... we're pretty tied up with the band and other projects that we're working on".

PAUL KENDALL

The decision to cease and desist from being a music journalist coincided with two contrasting possibilities. I was offered a job in the press office of a major record company. And my musician friends, having scored a deal as a duo with another big label, needed someone to look after their interests.

Since I was apparently the only person they knew and could trust, who was both literate and numerate, they asked if I would take on the role and let someone else do the bass playing when they toured. I was wavering, but in the end the decision was made for me. The press office job offer fell through (they hadn't got it signed off by the boss) and things were accelerating fast for John Otway & Wild Willy Barrett, so for the next year and a bit I became a band manager. A role for which I was not ideally suited, either by experience or temperament.

That year saw some significant highs – a medium-sized hit with '(Cor Baby That's) Really Free'; subsequent appearances on Top Of The Pops and The Old Grey Whistle Test (which became infamous when Otway leapt on top of his amp, only to take a nut-crushing tumble with legs akimbo on either side of it); a tour finale at a sold out Lyceum in London and an invitation to a party hosted by Paul McCartney, where we rubbed shoulders with members of Led Zeppelin and Keith Moon, on the night that he died. But it finished on the low note of a miserable tour round small venues in Scotland and Ireland, during an inclement winter. Such is the feast or famine reality of life in showbiz.

The one very good move I made, during my brief spell in band management, was to add merchandising to the tour planning. This wasn't unique in the music business – Brian Epstein had famously sold the Beatles' merchandising rights for next to nothing, back in the '60s, while Colonel Parker had profited handsomely from that part of the Elvis empire – but it was very unusual on our much lower rung of the stardom ladder. I lost count of the number of other managers, who shuffled up to me and made discrete enquiries about whether this was a worthwhile enterprise. It started off as a small-scale experiment: a modest collection of badges, t-shirts and posters, sold from a folding decorator's table in the foyer at gigs by the girlfriend of one of the entourage. But we almost ran out of stock on the first night of our post-hit nationwide tour of larger colleges and city halls, and I was frantically scrambling to get fresh supplies.

As it was my idea and I was organising everything, it had been agreed that the proceeds would be split equally between me and the artists. By the end of the tour, which was soon followed by my getting married, I'd made enough for a substantial deposit on our first flat and a nice honeymoon in France. The artists spent their share on a petrol-guzzling Jaguar and a photogenic but ageing Bentley, respectively. I guess that sums up why the business side of the music business usually ends up better off than the music side.

At the end of my final tour with the band, all the parties involved agreed that the future would be brighter, for everyone concerned, if we mutually accepted that we should go our separate ways. Leaving the frozen north and managerial duties behind me, I retreated, weary and disillusioned, to the sanctuary of our new marital home to consider how best to move forward.

Life, as John Lennon once noted, is what happens when you're busy making other plans. Purely by chance, this pondering coincided with a visit the very next weekend from a friend, who had been a bandmate during my college years. He'd already given up his musical ambitions and was now working as a copywriter at one of the top London advertising agencies. He made this sound like a perfect way to make decent amounts of money, while having indecent amounts of fun and shouldering minimal responsibility. I needed no further persuasion. As an alternative way of exploiting the one talent in which I felt something approaching complete confidence – writing – it seemed perfect. The job search took a few rounds of copy tests and interviews, but eventually I landed a spot at Young & Rubicam, which back then was the biggest ad agency in the world.

What followed was a thirty years long career as an advertising copywriter. (That's 'career' in the sense of veering all over the place, rather than any sort of planned or structured advancement.) I worked in agencies large and small, for clients large and small, and went from putting in unsocial hours for a pittance to putting in unsocial hours for something far better than a pittance. I accumulated a wall's worth of awards and, more importantly, a network of colleagues who became good friends and an invaluable source of mutual support, when the golden age of advertising lost its lustre from the '80s onwards.

My love of music hadn't diminished, by any means. In fact I rediscovered it, once my livelihood didn't depend on it. But active participation was confined to playing in various ad hoc bands at agency parties, being the go-to guy when ideas for songs to use in commercials were needed, and simply enjoying albums and gigs for their own sake.

Life as an employee came to an end in 2007, when the agency I was with at the time hired a budget-busting new creative director. Needing to make savings elsewhere on the payroll, I was the obvious target – the highest paid member of the department, when middle-aged and curmudgeonly was not the image they wished to project. I'd been finding it increasingly difficult to hide my impatience, during endless meetings with clients and account execs, most of them young enough to be my children, whose main priorities seemed to be self-preservation, ego projection and/or career advancement.

I wasn't sorry to go. The advertising business had become a lot less satisfying, as agencies went from being trusted advisers to hired drudges, and deadlines went from weeks to days and then hours, as we entered the digital age. The opportunity to do the best work, and chances to collaborate with film directors, photographers and other creative talents, had diminished correspondingly. The art director I was partnered with, during the final stretch of my agency life, didn't get to do a single photo or film shoot in our last year of our time together.

By this stage, however, the willingly carried responsibility of bringing home the bacon for a growing family had been lifted. All but the youngest of our four sons had been through college and were largely off the family payroll, while Tricia, my wife, had trained as a counsellor/psychotherapist and was making a significant contribution to our joint income. Which meant that, rather than being tied to a full-time job, I was able to go freelance and work as much or as little as I felt inclined or our needs required. So I chose not to pursue a (probably fruitless) search for another PAYE gig and embarked on a new freelance existence, which was not only more varied but gave me the possibility of exploring other avenues.

One of the things that came with this change of direction was commissions to provide 'content' for websites, which was where a rapidly increasing percentage of marketing spend was now going. Much of this work was for Canon, the world-leading camera company, and involved filming interviews with photographers and luminaries from the businesses that support and exploit them. This took me to some interesting places and put me in front of some interesting people. It also allowed me to develop the art of interviewing on camera. I'd conducted many interviews, back in my music journalist days, but doing it to be edited for a video requires an additional skill set to those needed for simply writing it up in print. What I learnt about putting your subject at ease in a potentially more pressurised situation, and leaving space for both interviewee and editor, was to prove invaluable.

I also got involved with the making of some corporate documentaries, which gave me a front row seat in observing how to go about this form of film production… and how not to. Again, lessons that would stand me in good stead for what was to come.

This paid work still left me with more free time than I'd had in many years, which I filled with a few attempts at writing scripts that extended beyond the confines of a 60 seconds commercial. For a while, it looked as if this might lead to something more tangible than rejection letters. When it didn't, my thoughts turned to combining my interest in film making with my love of music and developing a documentary about one of the musicians or groups I admired.

This was particularly inspired by a chap I knew, who'd been involved in producing a film about Arthur Lee and the band Love – a fine piece of work that's still available on DVD. They'd achieved this with minimal experience and resources, so I felt there was no reason why I shouldn't follow their example. Especially as I had a ready-made, very affordable crew to hand: #2 son Dan had studied photography at university, while #3 son Jack had done film making. Both were just venturing into the real world of work and they had been collaborating on making music videos for a number of bands.

The first issue was identifying a suitable subject. Many of the musicians or bands I would have most liked to document had already been done. Then fate, not for the last time, took a hand. Among the presents I was given for Christmas 2010 was 'Mr Tambourine Man', the Gene Clark biography written by John Einarson.

By the time I'd finished the book and revisited Gene's albums, I was convinced I'd found the right man. He'd died in 1991, but that was only one of many obstacles and inconveniences that I was either unaware of, at the time, or chose to ignore. Three decades of magnificent, mould-breaking music, combined with a compelling albeit tragic back story, made him irresistible. The long, strange trip was about to begin.

On stage at The Marquee in London c.1976, when my hair was much thicker and my waistline was somewhat thinner.

Interviewing Barry Masters of Eddie & The Hot Rods, backstage at Friars Aylesbury. (Chris France next to Barry, Pete Frame at back.)

Interviewing Lowell George of Little Feat for Zigzag magazine, at The Montcalm in London. Photo © Chalkie Davies.

With Otway & Barrett at Friars Aylesbury. Before I stopped being their bass player and started attempting to be their manager.

FIRST STEPS

By early January 2011, I'd finished reading the Gene Clark biography and was starting to give serious consideration to the possibility of making a film that, hopefully, would bring him at least some of the recognition that I felt he deserved. Gram Parsons (who I also like very much, it must be emphasised) had been getting nearly all the credit as the frontrunner in the pioneering of country rock aka 'cosmic American music', despite following in Gene's footsteps to a large extent. Gene was all but forgotten. Some of his albums, including the one that's now regarded as a lost classic, had even been out of print for a few years.

A quick trawl of the internet found no trace of any existing Gene Clark documentaries, other than ones involving his time with The Byrds. So it looked as if the path was clear, if not necessarily easy to navigate. I sounded out Dan and Jack about the idea and they agreed to go along with it. More out of filial loyalty, I suspect, than any particular enthusiasm for the subject or even belief that it would actually happen.

Jack - The first time you mentioned it was over dinner one day. The main thing I remember was that you hadn't spoken about it with Mum. She knew nothing about it. I was worried we wouldn't be able to get what you thought we'd be able to get. Whether you would have a different idea of what me and Daniel could do. Because we hadn't done our main videos at that point. We hadn't done the stuff with Swim Deep and Pixx and Maximo Park and others. We'd only done stuff with Cerebral Ballzy, which was pretty rough.

I'm more of a worrier than Daniel is. My memory is that Dan was like "Just let's do it". Which I was too. If nothing else, it would be an experience and a free holiday, to see some parts of America I hadn't seen before. I think I'd told you my concerns – that it wasn't going to look like an expensive, high-end documentary. It's not going to look like The Last Waltz. I still think you didn't know what to expect. But you at least tried to put my mind at rest that the limitations wouldn't matter, and that you knew it was going to be just two crew members with limited experience and cheaper cameras.

Dan - I remember being interested and excited about it. Apart from anything else, I was up for helping you do it, rather than thinking it was going to be good for me. I'd never heard of Gene Clark. And I don't think I bothered learning that much about him or listening to him, until we were actually on the road. I remember 'White Light' was my favourite, while we were travelling.

With the crew on board, we started thinking about the project in earnest. Even with an acknowledgement of the restrictions that would be imposed on us by our minimal funding and greenhorn status, we set out with a number of expectations and imperatives, which didn't really change along the way.

1) There would be little point in pitching it, at least in the early stages, to production companies, distributors, broadcasters or anyone else who might usually be involved in some aspect of documentary production. Even if we could get interest in such a niche proposition, it was highly unlikely that we, with our almost total lack of credentials, would be seen as the right people to pursue it. We would have to take it far enough to become inextricably involved and to demonstrate our capability before looking for support, financial or otherwise.

2) Even though it would significantly increase the cost of making it, the film would have to involve enough of the right interviewees and feature enough original music to make it credible. I'd seen too many music documentaries based on talking heads with plenty of opinions but no actual involvement with the subject(s) of the film, and which used a bare minimum of the music being discussed. There was even a Pink Floyd one which spoke with nobody directly connected to the band and contained not a single note of Pink Floyd music, opting instead to get someone to produce a soundtrack that sounded a bit like them.

3) We didn't want to use a scripted VO to carry the narrative. So the interviewees would need to cover the complete span of Gene's life and work, and we would need to be clear about which aspects of his story we wanted to include and what we needed to get from each of those interviewees, in order to tell it.

4) To make matters potentially even more budget-draining and logistically demanding, we wanted to capture the places where Gene had lived and worked. It seemed to me that those settings, both rural and urban, were a particular influence on him and were reflected through the contrasts in his music. And they were quite far flung, from the scenes of his formative years in Missouri to much of the considerable length of California. As it turned out, we had to go to (or very close to) all of those places to get the interviews we wanted, so the financial balancing act became irrelevant to a large extent. We just needed to make sure our schedule would allow time to shoot stuff other than interviews.

5) We would have to do it with the co-operation, or at least the blessing, of Gene's family and estate. Not only as a route to accessing family archives and establishing connections to potential interviewees, but to give our efforts legitimacy.

With all this in mind, my next move was to meet the guys who'd made the Arthur Lee/Love film, in the hope of picking up some tips from their experience of making a documentary as rookies, operating on a shoestring budget. Once the beers were set up, the first thing they told me was that they'd picked Gene Clark as the next subject for their company, Start Productions. Disappointment turned to relief, as they went on to say that they hadn't pursued this idea and were doing Mott The Hoople instead – another excellent piece of work, which is also still available on DVD. Just go to startproductions.net, if you'd like a copy.

Lucky Break #1

Although Start Productions had barely got out of the gate with their thoughts of doing a Gene Clark documentary, they had taken it as far as tracking down the lawyer, who was looking after Gene's estate on behalf of his two sons, Kelly and Kai. They very kindly gave me this chap's contact details and permission to use their names.
This can only be described as a flying start (no pun intended). I already knew that having Gene's family onside would be essential, if we were going to get maximum access to the people and material that would let us do the best possible job. We now had a key which would hopefully unlock that door.

The Start guys also shared some hard-earned wisdom about the pitfalls of dealing as film makers with musicians, their managers, record companies and publishers. Although, to be honest, after my own experience of navigating the music business as a musician, journalist and manager, and many years of arguing fine points of creativity with the corporate world as an advertising copywriter, none of this came as much of a surprise.

I felt reasonably confident about organising and executing the film making part of the project, but I knew there would be a lot of other work to be done. The various channels for exposing and distributing the film would need to be investigated and evaluated, and appropriate license deals would need to be arranged for the music and archive material that we wanted to include. This would almost certainly be the most expensive element, so it had to be done well. And it was some way outside my comfort zone and range of experience.

My secret weapon was Chris, an old friend who had spent much of his working life dealing with just such matters, as a promoter, as a manager and running his own label. I suckered him in with a free lunch in a sunny pub garden, while I explained the plan and why his help was needed. He agreed but, being a canny businessman, he asked for a percentage of the profits in return for his expertise and efforts. As I was quite certain that there wouldn't be any profits, I was happy to grant his request.

With this important element of the production seemingly in place, I moved on to assembling wish lists of songs we might want to use, so Chris could get underway with his licensing explorations, and of people we might hope to interview, so I could begin reaching out to them.

The interviewees

The people we ideally wanted to speak with, who were part of Gene's story and hopefully would be able to help tell it, were quite diverse in background, age and location. They included musicians he'd worked with, family and friends, and folk across the generations who were simply admirers. Some were considered must haves, some would be nice to have but not essential and some, frankly, were optimistic in the extreme. However, since our intention was to use only their words and occasional on-screen titles, without adding a narrated voiceover, getting a comprehensive range of good interviews was a basic requirement for achieving what we wanted to do with the film.

Identifying them was relatively straightforward, thanks to what I already knew and the book I'd just read. Tracking them down and getting in touch would be less so, even in the internet age. Some were still active and quite easy to reach, through third parties such as managers and agents if necessary. Others were more obscure or seemed to have disappeared off the radar. Old contacts from my distant music journalism days, and new ones being established as the project progressed, would be vital.

A fair few of the people who had been prominent in Gene's life were no longer with us. Michael Clarke, the drummer in the original Byrds line-up, who also played with Gene in several later ventures, had passed away in 1993; Jesse Ed Davis, producer of the magnificent 'White

Light' album, stumbled off this mortal coil in 1988; Thomas Jefferson Kaye, producer of the 'No Other' and 'Two Sides To Every Story' albums, and Gene's best buddy for several wild years in the '70s, made it as far as 1994; Terri Messina, Gene's on/off girlfriend for the last two decades of his life, died in 2007, leaving a trail of controversy and rumour in her wake. These were just some of the names that would have been on the wish list, had they not already joined Gene in the great dressing room in the sky.

Jim Dickson, the manager who guided The Byrds on their initial rush to stardom and was intermittently involved in Gene's solo career thereafter, was one of the first people we put on the list, but he died in April 2011, before we'd even finished compiling it. His death was a stark reminder that many of the people we hoped to speak with were getting on in years. It gave us a sense of urgency, which was both a helpful stimulant and, as events would prove, thoroughly justified. At the latest count, at least sixteen of the names that did appear on our final list couldn't be on it, if we were trying to make the film today.

Here's the list we drew up and how things panned out.

Musicians

Roger McGuinn, Chris Hillman, David Crosby – The three surviving original Byrds. They were right at the top of the must haves. If they didn't participate, the film would be lacking authenticity and gravitas from the start. I'd seen too many music documentaries where the principals were conspicuous by their absence, replaced by critics, so-called friends and others with only a tangential connection to the saga. But I was convinced that if we could get one of the three, the others would come aboard, if only because they wouldn't want to be left out or seem ungracious. This proved to be the case.
Chris, who had continued to work sporadically with Gene through his post-Byrds endeavours, and Roger both had their lives organised by

their wives, who responded positively to emails. David was surprisingly difficult to contact, having been through a number of different representatives in recent years, but we eventually got in touch with his current manager. Pinning each of them down to a time and place took a while, however, as their plans and inclinations fluctuated.

We ended up meeting Chris at his home in Ventura, a couple of hours up the coast from LA, which fitted in with our plans very well. Roger was due to tour the UK and Holland for several weeks in the autumn of 2011, but apparently had no available time to see us then, so we had to go to Florida at the end of our Stateside trip – a diversion which the budget could have done without. David, on the other hand, originally asked us to go to his home in California, but then decided he would rather fit us into his travels on a UK tour, which was happening as soon as we got back from the USA. This latter arrangement would give rise to some drama, which we'll get to later in the telling.

Doug Dillard, Bernie Leadon, David Jackson – Members of Dillard & Clark, the group that came together after Gene had left The Byrds. They made two albums in the late '60s, which were forerunners of what became known as country rock. The first one, 'The Fantastic Expedition of Dillard & Clark', remains one of my favourite albums to this day. Doug has always been regarded as one of the truly great banjo players, while Bernie went on to fame and fortune as a founder member of (The) Eagles. Only David – the least celebrated of the three – was eventually caught on film.

Doug and Bernie were both living in Nashville in 2011, which would have required yet another budget-stretching detour. We would happily have taken this, if we could get both of them. But Bernie, after a string of email exchanges, decided he didn't want to be interviewed. He'd been involved, a few years back, in the making of a documentary about Gram Parsons – another much mourned and even more self-sabotaging musical pioneer, who had been with him in The Flying Burrito Brothers. After a fair bit of to-ing and fro-ing via email, he finally sent me a message saying: "I am sorry to tell you this, but I just do not want to do this interview. I think the subject cannot be addressed by me without getting into the destructive tendencies and consequences… The Gram Parsons film was enough for me."

I'd already spoken on the phone with Doug, by this time, and sadly he was in very poor health. He was suffering from severe lung problems and died the following year. It was obvious, even from several thousand miles away at the other end of a transatlantic line, that there was no guarantee he'd be able to do an interview, if we did go to Nashville. So, with Bernie literally out of the picture, we regretfully concluded it was a risk we couldn't afford to take. We would have to rely on David Jackson to tell us about Dillard & Clark, along with the band's producer Larry Marks (see below). Thankfully, David still lived in the LA area and was willing to see us at his home in Van Nuys. He was also able to direct us to Doug Dillard's old house on Beachwood Drive, where Dillard & Clark had first assembled.

Barry McGuire – Barry was one of the leading lights in The New Christy Minstrels, probably the biggest group in America during the folk music boom of the early sixties. Gene's time with them covered the much shorter period between joining the group as an 18-year-old, after being discovered by them in a small Kansas City club, and leaving when the constant travelling got too much and they wouldn't offer an outlet for his own songs. Barry is best known for 'Eve Of Destruction', a huge solo hit in 1965, which coincided with The Byrds bursting onto the scene. He and Gene were also neighbours in Laurel Canyon for a while, as they both experienced the fruits of success.

Lucky Break #2

Barry was still touring, despite being in his late seventies, and was quite easy to get hold of, through the website that he ran. He was very gracious and happy to be involved. Even better, he was coming to Europe in May 2011 to play some shows with John York (see below).

This would give us an opportunity to do some filming earlier than expected, which proved to be crucial in getting the blessing of Gene's sons and estate.

Leland Sklar, Michael Utley – Two of the large crew of illustrious LA session players, who participated in the extraordinary 'No Other' album, which is generally regarded as Gene's masterpiece. Michael was also a major contributor to 'White Light' and 'Two Sides To Every Story'. Both proved quite hard to pin down, due to their very full schedules. As well as still being much in demand for session work, they were often away on tour – Michael as the musical director of Jimmy Buffett's band (he gets a name check on the song 'Volcano') and Leland with the likes of Phil Collins and Toto. Fortunately we were able to hook up with both of them during our narrow window of opportunity – Michael at his home in Venice Beach and Leland at his spectacular place outside Pasadena.

Carla Olson – Carla is a musician, songwriter and producer, who first came to prominence with The Textones in the late '70s. After being introduced to Gene at a gig in 1984, she partnered him in an all too brief renaissance of his recording career. Their 'So Rebellious A Lover' album was an early example of the primarily acoustic return to musical roots, which became known as Americana. They also made a live album, 'Silhouetted In Light'. We contacted her through her husband/manager, Saul Davis (see below).

John York and Pat Robinson – John had been with The Byrds for one year and a couple of albums, after all the original members apart from Roger McGuinn had moved on and before the original quintet got back together for the 1972 reunion album. But he had also played with Gene at different times: as a member of the very short-lived (just one weekend at The Whisky) Gene Clark Group in 1967; as part of the revolving line-up of 'Byrds tribute' bands, put together by Gene and Michael Clarke in the late '80s; and as the Y in CRY (Clark Robinson

York), a project which focused on songwriting and recording around the same time. Pat was a musician/writer/producer who made up the other third of that acronym. They had recorded a fair few new songs together, some of which saw the light of day after Gene's death. But they were always dogged by legal issues regarding ownership and most of those recordings have remained in the vaults.

We got in touch with John via Barry McGuire (see above) and interviewed them both during their European tour in May. He then put us together with Pat, who was also involved with Carla Olson and would join her, along with Saul Davis, to be interviewed in LA.

Bob Dylan – As one of the most reluctant interviewees on the planet, this was about as long as shots come. But we'd been given the email address of his manager, after being sworn to secrecy as to the source of that information, so we decided we'd give it a try. Especially as he was due to come to the UK in June and might have nothing better to do between shows. We also thought he might find it diverting to talk about a fellow artist who he apparently much admired, rather than being quizzed about himself. We got a very prompt, polite reply, telling us that the request had been forwarded to Mr Dylan but, as we already knew, he very rarely gave interviews so we shouldn't hold our collective breath. As things turned out, although it didn't get us a meeting with the great man, having that connection spared us a far more significant disappointment much later in the process of making the film.

Taj Mahal – Taj has been one of the foremost explorers of world music, along with Ry Cooder, his bandmate in The Rising Sons at the start of their long careers in the mid '60s. He didn't record or play any gigs with Gene, but he was a friend for many years and one of the celebs who came to support him at the last shows he played, shortly before his death. Taj was keen to share his appreciation of Gene for the film and, when we first spoke with his people, it looked like we'd be able to visit him at home in Berkeley, on our way up the Pacific Coast Highway. But then he started booking dates all over the country, during the time that we would be there. Most of them far away from our planned itinerary. The only connection that would be remotely practical was in Steelville, a quiet little place about 200 miles east of Kansas City, where we'd be heading to visit some of Gene's family and friends, and to check out the scenes of his upbringing. So that's where we met him.

Leon Russell – One of the most distinctive characters in music, Leon became recognisable worldwide when he led Joe Cocker's Mad Dogs and Englishmen band in 1970. Before that, he'd worked on numerous sessions, including Gene's first solo album. His grandiose string arrangement on 'Echoes' is especially noteworthy. Leon was now living in Tennessee, but was coming to Europe in both 2011 and 2012, and was touring extensively in the States during the autumn of 2011. We had a lengthy series of exchanges with his PR guy, who did his very best to be helpful, but sadly we were never able to find a suitable time and place in his schedule. The closest we came was a suggestion of going to Stavanger in Norway in March 2012, but that would have been (for us) a very expensive way of getting an interview which, with all due respect, wouldn't be central to the film. It would also have delayed the production process, while we waited to do it. (We naively imagined we'd be able to put the film together quite quickly, once we'd finished all the other filming during the autumn of 2011.)

Tom Petty – Tom was always open about his enthusiasm for The Byrds and their influence on him. And he covered Gene's 'Feel A Whole Lot Better' on 'Full Moon Fever' – the only song he himself didn't write on a multi-platinum selling album. I believe I was the first person in Europe to interview him, during my music journalist days, when The Heartbreakers came to the UK in 1977… Tom and the rest of the band, crammed into a small room in a cheap hotel in one of London's less desirable areas. I made much play of this in discussions with his management, suggesting (only half jokingly) that the good turn I'd done back then was now due to be repaid.

For some while it seemed he would give us a bit of his time while we were in California. He was between album recordings and tours in 2011, didn't appear to have any other notable commitments and was living in Santa Monica, close to LA. So we had reasons for optimism. Sadly we were told, quite late in the day, that Tom didn't do many interviews (even though there were plenty of examples, in print and on film, to contradict this) and wasn't going to be available. I couldn't help wondering if it was because he felt a bit awkward about the subject of Gene Clark. The sudden and substantial boost in Gene's income, which resulted from Tom's cover of 'Feel A Whole Lot Better', had funded his final drugs'n'booze binge, leading to talk of 'death by royalties'. Whatever the reason, not having Tom in the film would be one of our few real regrets.

Jon Faurot – Jon was part of the Mendocino scene and played with Gene at different times, over the last decade and a half of his life. He played bass in the band that did the residency at the Cinegrill on Hollywood Boulevard in 1991. Not long after that, it was Jon who found Gene's body in the kitchen of his home in Sherman Oaks, a suburb of LA. Jon was still living in Mendocino in 2011, but was hard to get hold of. The email address we managed to find didn't seem to be active (we were later told he didn't have an internet connection) and he didn't have anyone representing him. Eventually, through a friend of a friend, we were able to get a message through and he agreed to meet up while we were there. We also got his phone number, which made finalising arrangements a whole lot easier.

Chris Etheridge – Chris was the bass player in The Flying Burrito Brothers, with whom Gene was briefly involved, and played on the 'White Light' album. He was also one of the many musicians who moved to Northern California, away from the trials and temptations of LA, and his family became part of Gene's social circle in Mendocino. By 2011 he'd moved back to his hometown in Mississippi, which was way off our route map. We didn't even get as far as contacting him, as we were told he was seriously ill and wouldn't be going anywhere else that might make him more accessible. He passed away in early 2012.

Chip Douglas – Chip was a member of The Turtles during the peak of their career with 'Happy Together', and found even greater success as the producer of several of The Monkees' biggest hits. Between those two associations, he was in the group that Gene put together after leaving The Byrds. That didn't last long, like so many of Gene's projects, and broke up after a less than successful residency at The Whisky and abortive attempts at recording. (Their support band at The Whisky – The Doors – did rather better out of it.) We heard about another film maker, who was going to be interviewing Chip for something else, and he very kindly offered to ask questions for us, as well as for himself. Unfortunately the footage of that interview turned out to be completely inconsistent, visually, with what we shot and would have looked very odd, edited into our stuff. It didn't relate to a critical part of Gene's career either, so we never used it.

Peter Oliva – Another member of the Mendocino mafia, Peter played bass in The Mendocino Rhythm Section, which became The KC Southern Band. That was the band Gene brought to the UK in 1977, when I met and interviewed him. He was also in The Firebyrds, the touring group that Gene put together in the mid '80s. Peter went on to make several solo albums and had his own website, so was one of the easier targets to hit. He was more than happy to be invited to share his thoughts and memories, and was helpful in giving us contact details for other members of The KC Southern Band and people in Mendocino. He no longer lived there, having moved to Vacaville – about an hour north-east of San Francisco, so only a small detour from our direct route heading north. The other former band members were scattered across the country, however, as far afield as Iowa and Texas. So we didn't add them to this list.

Duke Bardwell – Duke had gone from playing bass for Elvis Presley's backing band in Vegas to the back of a knackered tour bus with The Silverados, the group that Gene put together after the release of 'No Other'. We assumed he would have some interesting stories to tell. As he was living in the northernmost part of Florida, a 10 hours' drive from Orlando, we couldn't get to him during our trip to the States, but another production company was making a documentary about him and generously agreed to shoot an interview for us. By the time that happened, we were able to provide reference to our shoots along with a list of questions, so they gave us footage of Duke that fitted in perfectly with the rest of the material.

Dan - The guys who did the Duke Bardwell shoot, they were obviously guys who knew how to film. Their lighting was a lot more subtle. They hadn't just pointed two lights at him and then tried to fix it after. I don't think we even diffused our lights, because they weren't powerful enough. If we'd diffused it, it would have knocked back whatever power we had.

Iain Matthews – Iain was one of the original members of Fairport Convention and then had a huge hit with a version of Joni Mitchell's 'Woodstock'. Over a career spanning many years and many albums, he's covered several of Gene's songs and certainly falls into the 'celebrity fan' category. It would have been nice to have him singing Gene's praises. But he lives in Holland and only visits the UK very occasionally. As with Leon Russell in Norway, we simply couldn't justify the cost of going there, to shoot something that wouldn't be a key part of the film. As a footnote, in 2014 Iain was one of the singers on the acclaimed 'No Other' tribute tour, which also featured members of Beach House, Grizzly Bear and Fleet Foxes. More about that when we get there.

Other music business characters

Larry Marks – Larry was a staff producer at Columbia Records and then A&M, in the mid to late '60s. He'd started to produce Gene's first solo album, when Columbia fired him before it could be finished. They'd become friends, however, so when he moved to A&M he was instrumental in getting Gene signed to that label and became the producer for Dillard & Clark. He'd gone on to work with a lot of other notables including The Flying Burrito Brothers, Helen Reddy and Liza Minnelli. Larry was another of the people on this list who was in poor health and he'd retired from the music business, so he wasn't easy to find. Our extensive trawling of the internet, however, came across a mention of him in a blog by a chap at an English university, who we reached out to. To our amazement, that resulted in our getting Larry's email address and a very gracious response from him. He told us: "I spent the better part of the mid to late '60s either in the studio or at the bar. Most of it with Gene." This subsequently led, by a somewhat circuitous route, to a connection with…

Jerry Moss – Jerry is the M in A&M Records, having set up the label in 1962, in partnership with bandleader Herb Alpert. The label hit the jackpot with acts such as The Carpenters, Peter Frampton and The Police, and was the most successful independent record company in the world for much of the 1970s and into the '80s. Gene Clark, being the most reluctant of stars, hadn't made a great contribution to that success, but Jerry seems to have gone above and beyond, in supporting and attempting to nurture him. Jerry was still very active, as a horse breeder and philanthropist, and we got a prompt reply to our first email message. "Gene was always a very positive and inspirational presence on our label", he said. "It would be a pleasure to revisit this time with you." We would meet at his Beverley Hills office.

David Geffen – Entertainment business mogul, who signed Gene to his Asylum label, following the Byrds reunion in 1972, and released the

'No Other' album. Gene blamed its lack of success on Geffen not promoting it properly, and allegedly tried to attack him in a Hollywood restaurant. Unsurprisingly, Gene was then dropped from the label. We tried several routes for getting a message to Mr. Geffen, but none of them got a reply. Of all the stars he's been involved with, Gene Clark probably isn't the one he remembers with the greatest fondness.

Al Coury – President of RSO Records, who signed Gene after he left Asylum and released the 'Two Sides To Every Story' album. Gene subsequently insulted Al and his wife during a business meeting in a Hollywood restaurant. He was dropped from that label too. We did get as far as speaking with Al's wife, Tina, but after initially being told that he would be "glad to give us an interview", he eventually decided that he couldn't remember anything about Gene Clark and had nothing to add to the telling of his story. It seemed that Gene's talent for sabotaging projects extended beyond the grave.

Saul Davis – When Gene teamed up with Carla Olson, who was and is his wife, Saul took over trying to manage him. He'd then been involved in attempts (some successful, some not) to put together a variety of posthumous releases, which seemed to have put him at odds with Gene's sons and estate. When we first got in touch, to ask about arranging interviews with Carla and himself, he alternated between being wary about any involvement and angling (as a good manager should) for a bigger role for Carla and some of his other clients, who had alleged connections to the Gene Clark saga. After a lot of exchanges, a good word from John York (see above) after we'd interviewed him in Germany and no little diplomacy, on our part, we not only got the interviews but some much appreciated help with sourcing archive material.

Bennett Glotzer – Was managing Tommy Kaye while he was producing Gene's 'No Other' and 'Two Sides' albums, and briefly tried to manage Gene during that period. He'd also managed Janis Joplin and Frank

Zappa, among others, for period of time. He wasn't available while we were in LA, but he was able to give us contact details for…

Al Hersh – Al had been tour manager during the last few years of The Byrds, including the making of the 1972 reunion album, and later for McGuinn Clark & Hillman throughout their brief lifespan. So he'd had a front row seat for events and exchanges that might euphemistically be described as 'interesting'. Al was one of several targets who hadn't yet embraced the internet world, but once we had his phone number, we were able to set up a meeting at his home in Topanga Canyon.

Ron Rainey – Was the booking agent for Roger McGuinn, when he went solo after disbanding The Byrds, and then for Roger and Gene as a duo. He was instrumental in putting together McGuinn, Clark & Hillman. He was out of the country while we were in the States, so we weren't able to get to him. He later turned out to be one of many folk who showed an interest in distributing/promoting the film, both during the making and after its completion. But, as with the other contenders, it never came to anything.

Family

Kelly and Kai Clark – Gene's sons, who spent quite a lot of time with him in LA during the '80s, after their parents separated. Although he's the younger brother, Kai seemed to have been more involved in trying to sustain Gene's legacy over the years, while Kelly took a back seat. At first we had to communicate with them through the lawyer who looked after Gene's estate, but once we'd managed to earn their trust, Kai was very open and helpful. He put us in touch with other family members and friends, and was an invaluable conduit to the family archives. Kelly was more reluctant to get actively involved, but was persuaded to give us an interview, which turned out to be one of the very best we got. Kai would meet us in Mendocino and be our guide while we were there. We met Kelly at his home in San Francisco, on our way up the coast.

Carlie Clark – Gene's wife and mother of Kelly and Kai. After their marriage broke down, Carlie went through some troubled times of her own. Once she'd recovered, she became an addiction counsellor. Kai arranged for us to meet her – originally in Mendocino but then she had some health problems and wasn't able to travel, so we were taken to her home in Auburn, near Sacramento.

David Clark and Rick Clark – Two of Gene's younger brothers, who had more contact with him than the rest of the family after he left Missouri. David seems to have been the closest of his siblings during their childhood and visited him in LA in the late '60s, while Rick was around in Mendocino and LA during the '70s. David was still living in Kansas City and although he was sceptical – suspicious even – at first, he agreed to meet with us to at least discuss the possibility of doing an interview. Sadly Rick was not in good shape at the time we were shooting the film and we were told he wasn't available. He made a recovery, however, and was able to join us when we had a screening in Mendocino in 2014.

Bonnie Clark Laible – Gene's older sister. She had left the family nest soon after finishing high school, to join the military, but would be important to an understanding of Gene's early life and the influences on him, and how Gene's celebrity and issues impacted on the rest of the Clarks. We met her together with David for an ice-breaking chat, when we first got to Kansas City, and interviewed them both at her home on the outskirts of town.

Friends

Jack Godden – Jack was Gene's best buddy during their teenage years around Kansas City, watching his growth as a musician and songwriter, up to the point where his life would be transformed overnight by The New Christy Minstrels.

Lucky Break #3

While trawling the internet for anything Gene-related, I stumbled across an article in a Kansas City newspaper about a local author/film maker, who was doing some work on Gene's early life. I got in touch, hoping to get some information and maybe some contacts. We got much more. Dan Torchia became our man in Kansas City and a priceless part of the project. (Literally 'priceless'... Dan threw himself into it, as we were doing, simply because he felt strongly about Gene and the music. Payment for all his time and effort never came into it.) He not only liaised with the people we wanted to interview, he sorted out equipment hire at mate's rates, helped source archive material, identified the right locations and was our guide while we were in town. He even recommended where we should stay and where we should eat. We could have done it without him, but it would have been a lot harder, far less productive and nowhere near as enjoyable. Thanks again, Dan.

Through Dan Torchia, an interview with Jack Godden was arranged. He was waiting for a heart operation when we visited him at his home and he passed away not long afterwards. One of too many interviewees who we got to in the nick of time. Dan also opened up the possibility of interviewing Joe Meyers and Jimmy Glover, two of Gene's bandmates from his teenage Kansas City days. But they were further afield and we would have used up a lot of our limited time in Missouri getting to them. We decided to prioritise meeting with Gene's family members and capturing the various locations around Kansas City that were part of the story or would capture the atmosphere of his early years.

Tom Slocum – A musician and songwriter, who was briefly married to Emmylou Harris (small world!). Tom knew Tommy Kaye and was summoned to Mendocino, when Tommy and Gene were putting a new band together after making the 'Two Sides' album. Tom never joined the band, but he remained one of Gene's closest friends for the rest of his life. Although we made email contact with him early on, pinning him down to a time and place for an interview proved tricky, as he seemed to have no fixed abode, following the break-up of his most recent marriage, and he kept changing his email and Facebook accounts. We finally got to him at a house in Santa Barbara. We thought it was a friend's place, but were never quite sure.

Michelle Phillips – Of The Mamas & The Papas. She and Gene had a brief fling in 1966, while she and her husband/bandmate John Phillips were going their separate ways. It was kept secret at the time, and only became public knowledge when Michelle wrote her autobiography in 1986. We had a connection to her through Tom Slocum. But there were plans to make a documentary about her, and we were told she wanted to keep her recollections for that project and "at this point in time couldn't commit to any further discussion re Gene Clark".

Ken Mansfield – Ken should probably be in the 'Music business characters' section of this list, as he had a long and varied career in the industry, as a record company executive (he worked with Apple Records and was one of the handful of people on the roof of The Beatles' Savile Row offices, when they did their famous last performance) and as a producer in Nashville, for artists such as Waylon Jennings and Willie Nelson. In fact he'd probably be worth a documentary in his own right. But his involvement with Gene was purely as a friend. They met when Ken joined the exodus to Mendocino in the mid '70s and also spent time together back in LA. Ken later found God, becoming a motivational speaker and writer. Tom Slocum gave us his email address and we got a prompt, positive reply – "Gene and I had a special and personal relationship. I am glad you are going to take this look at his life. I will be happy to participate." Ken was living in Murphys, California at the time. A reasonably convenient point on our way back south to LA, after our journey round the northern parts of the state. Soon after he moved to the top end of Florida, almost into Alabama, which would have been a lot less accessible.

Philip Oleno – Philip and his wife Ea had probably been Gene and Carlie's closest friends, during their Mendocino years. Philip, who shared digs with Jim Morrison's at film school, became a woodworker and metalsmith. Ea had been a Hollywood hairdresser and created the styling for the cover of the 'No Other' album. She had passed away quite recently, and we were told that Philip had been hit very hard by the loss. There was no guarantee he would want to be interviewed, but Kai said he would take us to visit, while we were in Mendocino, and we would have to hope for the best. He was one of many folk who were sympathetic to the low key, 'labour of love' nature of the project and ended up giving us a moving, if somewhat rueful account of Gene and Carlie's Mendocino years.

He also had a visit from a friend, Garth Beckington, while we were with him. Garth had been the guitarist in the ill-starred Cinegrill band, so we sat him down in front of the camera and got an interview that we hadn't planned for. My now comprehensive knowledge of the Gene Clark story paid off, however, and I was able to conduct an impromptu quiz/conversation with a reasonable awareness of Garth's place in it.

Pamela Des Barres – A member of the Zappa-inspired GTOs (Girls Together Outrageously) and a prominent figure on the LA music scene in the '60s and '70s. She'd had a lengthy relationship with Chris Hillman, so was part of Gene's orbit and would no doubt have given us some colourful background to that period of the story. We contacted her through her website and she would have been happy to give us an interview, but she was away from home during the time we were in LA and wasn't available. You can't win 'em all.

Others

Sid Griffin – Something of a Renaissance Man, Sid first made his name with The Long Ryders, who were at the forefront of the so-called Paisley Underground scene in the early '80s. Which was where he got to know Gene. Sid had become a prolific author and broadcaster, while continuing his music career with The Coal Porters and as a solo artist. He had played a significant part in keeping Gene's flame burning over the years, through organising and participating in re-issues and compilations. Conveniently he'd been living in London for many years. However, he was wary of getting involved at first, due to apparent issues with both the estate and the Saul Davis camp. He was concerned that his presence might jeopardise our relationships with them. Once these concerns were laid to rest, Sid became a true friend to the project, not only giving us an excellent interview but providing invaluable and unexpected assistance in other ways.

Johnny Rogan – Author of many magisterial volumes about musicians, including Ray Davies and Van Morrison, not least his multi-part Byrds epic. Johnny avoided 21st century channels of communication and guarded his privacy zealously. But he'd also written for *Zigzag* back in the day and we had several friends in common, so the drawbridge was lifted. He was a key interviewee as well as a great source of information, advice and contacts. He passed away, suddenly and unexpectedly, while this book was being written. He's much missed.

John Einarson – John was the author of 'Mr Tambourine Man', the Gene Clark biography that triggered this whole project. Few people know more about Gene's life and its many twists and turns. But there were two problems – 1) He lives in Winnipeg, so was nowhere near where we would be going, and 2) We weren't able to make email contact with him until after we'd finished shooting. When we did finally get through to him, he was helpful in sourcing archive material. But the telling of Gene's tale had to be left to others.

Reaching out

With a preliminary wish list assembled, I then put together a basic proposal document, to share with Gene's estate and sons in the first instance, and then with anyone else – proper production companies, distributors etc – who we might try to get involved at a later stage.

Gene Clark Documentary

A proposal

The Idea

Our intention is to make a feature length documentary
that pays tribute to the work of Gene Clark and tells his
story.

That story will be told through newly-filmed interviews
with the people who knew him best - family, friends and
fellow musicians - and with those who admire his work. We
also expect to source existing audio interviews with Gene
himself and others.

It will be illustrated with: interviewees talking, in
various appropriate locations; archive film; archive
photography; and new footage of the places where Gene
lived and worked.

Most importantly, it will showcase Gene's music, from all
stages of his career. Including his recordings with The
Byrds, but with the emphasis on those he made after
leaving that band.

Once completed, we would aim to show the film at film
festivals, make it available to TV stations in various
territories and release it on DVD.

The Story

Gene's story naturally follows a classic dramatic arc:
success (on a massive, international scale), followed by
struggles (professional and personal), finally achieving
redemption - in this case, in the form of the continuing
growth in Gene's reputation and appreciation of his work,
since his death.

His early years and his rise to fame and fortune with The
Byrds will be naturally be covered, but not at undue
length, as the main focus of the film will be on what
followed and the work that is less well known.
It will not be possible to tell the story honestly
without mentioning Gene's ambivalent attitude to stardom
and success. But the primary focus throughout will be on
the music and the making of it - especially Gene's
collaboration with Doug Dillard, and the 'White Light'
and 'No Other' albums.
When dealing with the posthumous story, the film will
concentrate on the recognition that Gene and his work
continue to earn, rather than on the controversies and
legal battles that ensued. It will also reference the
wealth of unreleased material waiting to be tapped.

The Interviewees
Family:

Kelly Clark	Kai Clark	Carlie Clark
David Clark	Bonnie Clark Laible	Rick Clark

Musicians:

Roger McGuinn	Chris Hillman	David Crosby
Doug Dillard	Carla Olson	Bernie Leadon
Michael Utley	Barry McGuire	Leon Russell
Chris Ethridge	Leland Sklar	Peter Oliva
John York	Pat Robinson	Duke Bardwell

Friends and associates:

David Geffen	Jerry Moss	Jim Dickson
Sid Griffin	Johnny Rogan	John Einarson
Philip O'Leno	Tom Slocum	Saul Davis
Michelle Phillips		

Famous Fans:

Bob Dylan	Robert Plant	Tom Petty
Ian Matthews	Taj Mahal	

The People

Paul Kendall - Is a full-time writer and part-time
musician. In the 1970s, he worked for various music
publications, most notably *Zigzag* magazine. He met Gene
during the 1977 UK tour with McGuinn and Hillman, and
interviewed him at length. He went on to a successful
career in advertising with a number of major
international agencies, and has been creative director on
more commercials and corporate films than he can
remember. He is now in the happy position of being able
to return to his first loves and concentrate on the
projects closest to his heart.

Jack Kendall - Is a film maker, editor and scriptwriter.
In addition to making music videos, he creates corporate
films for clients such as Canon Europe and Visa Pour
L'Image (the world's biggest photojournalism festival).

Chris France - Has over three decades of experience in
the music business. He ran the Music of Life label for
many years (giving Prince his only Number One single in
the UK) and currently administers the musical legacy of
The Small Faces. He also co-produced the Run DMC
documentary *Walk This Way*, which was shown on MTV.

Funding

The project will initially be self-funded. An adequate
budget is in place for shooting interviews and other
footage, in the UK and the USA, and for post-production.

If you actually know about such things, this will no doubt seem extraordinarily naïve and inadequate. Particularly on the financial side. But we were making it up (and would hopefully be learning) as we went along. I did run it past a couple of people, who knew the Gene story and some of the characters in it, to see if we were striking any wrong notes and if they had any suggestions for more interviewees. But they weren't qualified to judge it as a serious proposal for film production.

Nevertheless we were anxious to press on, before anyone else on our interviewee list died. So I fired it off, attached to an email to the estate's lawyer:

Dear Mr Johnson
I've been given your email address by friends who run Start Productions – the company who made the *Love Story* documentary, about Arthur Lee and Love. I believe they spoke with you about the possibility of doing a similar film on Gene Clark.
They were unable to pursue that project, but I found out about it when I had a similar idea and picked their brains to learn from their experience of making the Love film.
My ambition is to make a film that pays tribute to Gene and his work, which I believe deserves a much wider audience. A shooting budget is available, along with the skills and resources needed to execute this ambition to a high professional standard and with an informed, sympathetic approach. The attached proposal will give you more details of the intentions and the credentials of the people involved.
We would like to pursue the project on an authorised basis with the blessing and, ideally, the co-operation of the people closest to Gene. Not least because we know this will give us a better end result.
I look forward to hearing your thoughts, once you've had a chance to consider the attached. If you have any questions about any aspect of the project, please don't hesitate to ask.
Kind regards
Paul Kendall

I got an immediate response, but only to say that the proposal would be discussed with Kelly and Kai. Several weeks went by before, after a bit of chasing, I got an invitation to go and meet them in Los Angeles at the end of April. Kai would be playing there with his band, to mark the reissue of his father's 'Two Sides To Every Story' album. I would have loved to take up the offer, but since the excursion would have wiped out a significant chunk of our notional budget, I gracefully declined. Which prompted this reply:

Paul

As I mentioned, the Clarks are generally receptive, but you are not the first filmmaker to "pitch" a biopic about Gene Clark, and the history has been that there is a lot of excitement and an effort to generate a lot of excitement with the family, and then not much happens. I think you mentioned that you got my contact information from other filmmakers who at one point were pitching something very similar to what you are presenting now. So, I would say that you should proceed with the assumption that there is initial support from the Clarks for the concept, and that as you concretize things and have funding committed, distribution or festival plans in place, etc. etc. you could keep us in the loop. At the point where you need actual assistance, whether it's access or whatever, that is where you will have to be clear and convincing that this is something that will happen and that it will be a worthy production.

Scott

This didn't come as a surprise. I knew our lack of credentials and resources would inspire doubts in anyone we approached about the film. But I had a cunning plan up my sleeve. While waiting to hear back from the estate I'd kept busy, doing research into the various people we wanted to interview and the existence of relevant archive material.

In the course of doing this research, I'd discovered that Barry McGuire, who had been in The New Christy Minstrels when they gave a teenage

Gene Clark his big break and took him away from home, would be touring Germany and The Netherlands in May. I'd also found some local newspaper articles about the Kansas City music scene in the early '60s and some clips of old TV shows, which had Gene performing with The New Christy Minstrels. If we interviewed Barry, we could do a basic assembly of that chapter of the film. This would hopefully demonstrate to the Clarks that we were a) serious about making the film, and b) competent to do it. There would obviously be some expense involved in going across The Channel to film Barry, but I was confident we could keep costs to a minimum and that doing it would be a good trial run for myself, Jack and Dan. (The Clarks and their lawyer weren't the only ones who had some questions about whether we were up to the job!)

Lucky Break #4

Before we headed to Germany to meet up with Mr McGuire, I had another journey to make. Down to Surrey, to meet another Barry – Barry Ballard, who was introduced via an old Zigzag connection. He was one of the world's top two Byrds archivists (we'd be connecting with the other one in due course), so I was hopeful he'd be able to provide some valuable stuff for the film.
My hopes were exceeded, to put it mildly. He not only had a wealth of recordings, photos and cuttings, as I'd expected, he also brought out a collection of cassettes containing interviews which had been done back in the '70s, with Gene and others connected to his story, such as Tommy Kaye. The tape of my own interview with Gene had disappeared years before – something I now hugely regretted – so these were going to be a massive contribution, allowing us to hear from people who were central to the story but no longer with us. What leaped out, however, were some home movie recordings, which had been shot by Tom Slocum. One showed Gene playing live at a small club, during the '80s, with one of the Byrds Tribute line-ups. Even more thrilling was film of Gene and a group of friends, sitting

round his kitchen table, doing a somewhat ramshackle but very moving rendition of Dylan's 'I Shall Be Released'. Knowing Gene's story as I did, my heart skipped a beat as soon as I saw it. We had the ending to our film before we'd even started shooting it.

Barry promised to make copies of everything and I headed home in the highest of spirits.

GETTING IT TOGETHER PT.1

Taking precautions

As soon as word about our project started spreading among family and friends, we got advice from several sources, which strongly suggested we should set up a limited company to front it.

Limited companies are all too often used by unscrupulous operators, who use them as a way to make money while running up debts, for which they aren't personally responsible once they've dissolved the company. We had no such intentions, but – given the licensing minefield we would be entering into and the complexity of Gene's recording and publishing arrangements – we were persuaded that we should protect ourselves against the possibility, however remote, of inadvertently getting into a costly copyright dispute.

Having a limited company would inevitably involve costs we could do without, both in setting it up and in submitting the necessary annual reports. But we (or rather I) decided that it was worth it, to be able to sleep easy at night.

Once that decision was made, the first thing we had to do was come up with a name for the company. A load of ideas were batted around before we settled on Four Suns Productions. I felt this was well omened, as it reflected both the fact that I had four sons and the four things that I think of as the primary lights of my life – my family and friends, music, books and the beauties of nature. All of which would play a significant part in the making of the film.

The next order of business was devising a logo for the company. To go on a letterhead and, hopefully, on the finished product in whatever form it might take.

After more than thirty years in advertising, I knew a good array of art directors and designers who I might be able to call on for assistance with this. My first port of call was a guy called Andy Mawson. Andy was not only very talented but also a good friend, who I felt might be persuaded to do a favour. On top of that, he had not long stepped away from the advertising business to run an art gallery and framing business in the lovely seaside town of Whitstable. So I felt he might be more inclined to devote some mind space and a few hours of his time to something that was no longer his day job.

Sure enough, Andy did us proud and very soon started sending over a range of ideas.

FOUR SONS

PRODUCTION.

FOUR · SUNS PRODUCTIONS.

After some discussion and fine tuning, this is what we ended up with.
We were very pleased with it.

**FOUR SUNS
PRODUCTIONS**

While this was going on, our accountant was handling the more prosaic job of registering Four Suns Productions Ltd as a legal entity and I bought domains for foursunsproductions.com and foursunsproductions.co.uk, along with email accounts for myself and Chris. By the end of July 2011, we were good to go. An actual website and a Facebook page would come later.

The gear

Technology really isn't my thing, so I was very much in Jack and Dan's hands when it came to deciding what we would need, in order to shoot something that would go some way towards matching our cinematic aspirations without wildly exceeding our very limited budget.

One thing I did know, from my work with Canon, was that they'd brought out a new DSLR (digital single lens reflex) camera, which was a complete game changer. The EOS 5D Mark II was the first stills camera that could also shoot HD film. There were obviously some things it couldn't do, which film cameras could. But for our project, it had the supreme virtues of being easily portable and relatively affordable. It was also far more discreet than a film camera, so it wouldn't arouse any awkward questions when going through customs or getting location footage.

Jack - There were obviously loads of limitations with the 5D, particularly in terms of movement because of the interlacing. Every time you moved it, it went all wavy.

Dan - They say "The best camera is the one you have on you". We wouldn't have known what other camera to get. We were quite technically unaware at that point. I've never been that technical and I'm not interested in the technicalities of digital cameras, especially. When I was shooting live stuff, other photographers would come up and ask me about lenses and so on. I couldn't give a f***. I have literally no interest in that side of things. It's just the one I have. I know the focal length and that's about it. I don't have any interest in digital lenses. You can get better cameras, but I wouldn't have known what to get at that point. You have to work with what you've got. And we didn't have the know how or the budget or the time to over-complicate things. We had what we had and we used it.

We needed two of the cameras, both to give us more options when shooting and so we would have back-up in the event of technical issues. For the first bit of filming in Europe, which took only a few days, I was able to borrow them from Canon, along with a choice of lenses. To do the long trip around the States, however, we had to buy them. Fortunately, as the Mark II been on the market for a couple of years and an updated version was imminent, good quality second-hand models were available at prices that were quite a lot lower than for new ones. Dan had some lenses already, which were compatible with the Mark II, and we bought a couple more, including a 70/200, which he thought would be helpful.

Dan - This is how little we knew about the technical stuff. With most decent cameras, when you shoot you shoot raw, so that it's quite a flat image. And then you pull and push stuff afterwards. So when we first shot something that Alex Berry graded – it might have been the 'King City' video for Swim Deep – I remember him saying that there's this setting, I think they call it LUT, you have to download it. It's called Cinestyle. Because on those 5Ds, the early ones, they shot it with a look already added. The blacks were already very black and the whites were already very white. With those digital SLRs there's a very definite look to it. Probably the newer ones are better now, but you can definitely tell when something is shot on one of those, because it's so contrasty and looks so digital. I knew how I wanted stuff to look, but I couldn't get it to look like that.

So we got ourselves equipped with cameras, lenses and other accessories, but still needed a lighting rig that would allow us to shoot interviews in a variety of settings and to a passably professional standard. For the Barry McGuire shoot in Germany and for the ones we did at home, later in the year, we were able to hire a three lights rig at quite reasonable prices from a very good company, just a half hour's drive from home.

When we went to the States, things got a bit more complicated. The local hire companies, of which there were many, as you'd expect in the film-making capital of the world, were not only more expensive (we wanted to keep the gear for a couple of weeks, as we wandered the length and breadth of California) but had insurance issues with non-American customers. Basically the hirer has to provide their own insurance in the States – which the hire company does for you in Europe – and American insurance companies either wouldn't touch non-residents or demanded a ludicrous premium. Fortunately (a word that crops up regularly in this saga) a friend of a friend of a friend had put us in touch with a very genial Geordie ex-pat in LA, who had the perfect set-up and was willing to let us take it on the California leg of our travels it at a very good rate plus a refundable deposit.

For the shoots in Kansas City, our man Dan Torchia borrowed a rig from a friend for a few days, at what were very much mate's rates. He even brought it to the airport when we arrived at crack of dawn, bless his heart. Which just left the one day of filming in Orlando with Mr McGuinn, for which we found a local lighting guy who was able to do the job.

We'd already decided how we would shoot all the interviews – one fixed camera, directly in front of the interviewee, which would film continuously, with breaks to change the memory card as needed; Dan roaming round the periphery, getting different angles with the other camera; and Jack holding the boom with the mic on it. I would sit alongside the fixed camera, conducting the interviews and keeping an eye on the memory card capacity.

Jack - In 'The Last Waltz', the film about The Band's farewell concert, directed by Martin Scorcese, he didn't have a locked off camera at all for the interviews. Even the main camera was slightly handheld. You can see there's a bit of movement to it, which looks nice. I wanted to emulate that, but with the 5D rather than a high end film camera, which he was using in the '70s, it just looked way too wobbly.

What I wish we'd done now was just locked off both. By the time we did Roger McGuinn, which was our last interview in America, and we were doing it in our hotel room, I put the camera on a pillow. That was a bit better. I had a pillow resting on my leg and then the camera resting on the pillow. So there's slight movement, but it's a bit more stabilised. But with some of the others I wasn't able to do that and I was in uncomfortable positions, just holding it with my hand, and it's really shaky.

We could barely use any of that B camera from the interviews. Most of it was unusable. Which was OK, because we weren't really using any of the shots long enough to have to cut back and forth. And we ended up with enough archive material that I could cut away to, which I would have wanted to do anyway. The B camera was only ever as a back-up. When there were times when we cut words out, or an umm, and I wanted to let that flow just on their face, I would have to cut to the B camera. It looks OK in the Roger McGuinn interview, where I was able to rest it on a pillow. But in the end I don't think the little bit of nice movement we got was worth sacrificing being able to cut back to that B camera as much as we might have wanted in the earlier ones.

I wish we'd just locked off both of them. But again, that was me not knowing enough about that camera at the time.

Dan - Our sound recording was about as basic as you could get – a mic plugged into Jack's Sony DV camera. It's not an immersive experience. But it's not crackling, the levels are fine. I'm sure a sound designer would say "It's the most basic sound I've ever heard". But it's clear and it's clean enough. Most people, unless they're professionals of some sort, are more interested in the story. So unless it's intolerably bad, unless it looks so shit that it's unwatchable, you're more likely to accept bad filming. But you can't accept bad sound. If you're watching something and it's not the best lighting you've ever seen, then people quickly get over that if the story's carrying it. If the sound's bad, then it's "I can't watch this".

Jack - I recorded from my boom mic into my Sony tape camera, so it's all on tape. The audio was all from a Sony boom mic – a good Sony boom mic – into quite an old mini DV camera. Then I didn't really do much touching up to it afterwards. I tried to do a little bit, but I'm not a sound guy, so I didn't really know what to do with it. I played with the levels slightly and balanced it all out, and there was so much mixing with music anyway, so maybe it didn't really matter. But I wonder if some people would watch it and go "Oh yeah, the treble on that or the high balance on that audio is awful". I don't know. If it was now, I think I'd say "Let's get a sound guy". But in the end it didn't matter and we haven't had any complaints about that.

Dan - If we'd taken another person – a sound guy or a cameraman – I think they'd have got stressed with us. "What the fuck is this I've signed up for? This isn't a professional shoot." I seriously think that's what would have been said. "Who the fuck are these guys? They're chancing it." Which is what we were doing. We'd have been asking a professional sound guy or lighting guy to set up in a few minutes. We didn't understand, at that point, how long it should take to do things. We didn't know enough to say "Look, I know you're trying to do this, but let's swap it out for that, because we don't have time." All we could have said was "Be quicker". Or "I want it to look like this", but with no reference to how to make it look like that. It would have been "None of us know what we're doing, just make it happen and be quick, please". It certainly wasn't a professional set up. We were using lights that you'd usually just use for focus or in a theatre thing. You wouldn't really use them to light a professional shoot. And the cameras would probably be used for B roll, not for the actual interviews. We were definitely learning as we went. Totally learning as we went.

We wanted to have a different setting for each interview (not that we'd have much choice, as they'd be shot in a wide variety of locations) but we wanted to use lighting to give them some consistency of look.

In the end the interviews were all shot with a 85mm lens at f2.8 and with a variety of lighting rigs, although they were all broadly similar. We mostly used a soft light from the front with a second one from behind, giving a highlight. Another light was sometimes needed to give more information on the background but that depended on where we were filming. Some interviews took place indoors, some outdoors and a couple with no ambient light at all.

Dan - I'd probably been on more film shoots than Jack, in terms of being on music video shoots or shooting stills when they were filming a music video. And I pay attention to that kind of thing, so I had an idea in my head of how things go and what's meant to be done. And obviously I did photography as well. I don't overly light stuff, or even use extra lighting at all if possible, when I'm doing my photo shoots. My style, I guess, even if you're using lights is to make it look natural, like daylight. I don't put in a light source if it doesn't make sense. But I had no real experience and I would definitely have done it differently now. If I was drawing up a lighting list now, based on the same cost and the same amount of space, it would be a lot different. But then I'd actually know what I was talking about these days. And I could definitely have sourced different lighting options. But we worked with what we had.

As I would with all the interviews, I prepared a list of questions for each subject, taking into account their relationship with Gene and their involvement in or knowledge of his story. Having a clear idea of what we needed to get out of each interview was fundamental to actually getting it. But I also wanted to allow for spontaneity in pursuing information or lines of thought that weren't necessarily expected, and to make the exchanges feel like a relaxed conversation rather than a rigid Q&A session.

Dan - You know how to interview people. You've done it for however long. And you knew about those people and a lot about that kind of stuff. So that obviously helped. Jack, for all his technical unawareness, has watched a lot of films and documentaries, so does know how to block stuff out. He knows what's going to look right, in terms of where it's sitting. And he knows how to edit that sort of stuff pretty well. He wouldn't be able to do something completely out of the ordinary with an edit, but to put stuff together... he understands the pacing of stuff. He's very much a film maker who's watched a lot of stuff, so is able to store that and emulate the pace and the blocking.

Jack - It wasn't until we did the 'King City' video with Swim Deep that we started working with other people, and me and Dan started learning about other lenses and other cameras.... what was the best technical equipment to use. When we did the Gene Clark film we didn't really know and I don't think Dan had spoken to many professional directors of photography. So he was just going off his photography experience, rather than his film making experience. Now I think about it, maybe Daniel was relying on me more than I knew, to know about film making and the technical side of things. Maybe he was thinking "I'll just do the lighting set up for the interviews and everything else is up to Jack".

The crucial first shoot

Barry McGuire and John York's visit to Europe, in May 2011, gave us a perfect opportunity to shoot a couple of interviews at a very early stage of the project. This proved to be instrumental in getting Gene's sons and his estate onside and it also allowed us to give our film making process – the equipment and how we would use it – a trial run, before considering the far more extensive and intensive (and expensive) demands of a lengthy trip round the States.

We liaised with their European agent, a very amiable and helpful Swiss chap, and arranged to meet them in Frankfurt, where they would be performing at the birthday party of a wealthy fan. The fan not only invited us to join the party, but agreed we could film some of the performance.

Jack - I knew that, going into Germany, the main thing was going to be doing the interviews. We were shooting around the concert that they did. But all we went out there to do was shoot the two interviews and, as a bonus, film the gig and see if we could do anything with that. I think the only issue I would have had, going into that, was the sound and whether that was going to be good enough. But we'd done something similar in Perpignan in France, at the Visa Pour L'Image photojournalism festival, so I was probably reminded of that and Dan was like "Oh, we can do it this way and that way". And I was like "The lighting is Dan's issue and if that falls apart, it's his fault". So I don't remember being worried, when we were going into the Barry McGuire and John York stuff.

To keep costs to a minimum, we decided we would drive direct to Frankfurt, setting off at crack of dawn to arrive in time for the party and performance in the evening, shoot the interviews the next morning and then come straight back. This would minimise both the period for hiring the lighting rig that we were taking with us and what we'd spend on eating and sleeping. The downside was non-stop journeys of more than 500 miles each way on successive days.

We nearly fell at the first hurdle. As we travelled round the M25, en route to an early rail crossing through the Channel Tunnel, we hit a massive tailback and then a diversion, following an incident of some sort. We eventually reached the Tunnel ninety minutes late, having missed our booked time. To our great relief, as it was mid-week in a quieter time of year, we were able to get on another shuttle quite quickly and a speed limit busting dash across France, Belgium, the Netherlands and Germany got us to Frankfurt just in time to find the party venue, say hello to Barry and John, and set up ready for action.

The show that the duo put on, called 'Trippin' The Sixties', was a very engaging mix of storytelling and songs from that golden age. Barry had been buddies with most of the main characters in Los Angeles, as it became the epicentre of the American record business from the mid '60s onwards, and he did their hits as well as his own, with The New Christy Minstrels and as a solo artist. We filmed Barry singing 'Green Green', the Christys' first big hit, which ended up allowing Jack to edit a very nice segue into an archive clip of the group doing the same song on a TV show, with Gene lurking sheepishly to one side.

Jack - We must have known, at least before the day, that we were going to shoot the gig, because I remember getting that specifically for the film. It's the only stuff from the Frankfurt concert that we used, where I transitioned from Barry McGuire singing now to him with the New Christy Minstrels. And we must have known before we went out to Germany, because you were able to show me that clip and we were waiting specifically for that song, so we could transition from him now to him singing that same song back then. So we must have already seen that footage. I knew exactly which angle to shoot it from as well.

The next day we filmed interviews with Barry and John in a conference room at our hotel. Not the ideal setting, but the only viable option at short notice. Fortunately we'd brought a few props with us, so were able to dress the 'set' to make it a bit more interesting. And our intention, from the start, was to have a shallow depth of field.

Jack - I remember what you particularly wanted... because you didn't really give us much, you kind of let us think of our own references and shoot it our own way...what you wanted was that kind of abstract – it's called 'bokeh' – where it's all blurred out in the background. Which we weren't able to get a lot of the time, with the lenses we had. We would have needed different lenses. We were able to get it sometimes. It became an issue straight away, in Germany. Because of the room, Barry wasn't far enough away from the background to make the background be out of focus, when we had it sharp and in focus on him, with the lenses we had. And that came up in quite a few instances. With John York it did work, because we shot the other way, down the room, and we put his guitar as far away as possible, really far in the background and it was out of focus. But when we were going around in America, a lot of the rooms were quite small. With Bonnie and David Clark it was basically her kitchen. So there were some examples where the background wasn't really out of focus. It was flatter than we would have wanted it to be. Certainly flatter than you would have wanted it, from what you were saying beforehand. But that was all because of the lenses and that was Daniel's department. Either the lenses didn't exist or he didn't know enough about other camera lenses.

Dan - The lighting wasn't that considered. It was literally "OK, he looks lit, he's showing up on camera, there's a little bit of shape…we're not completely side lit, like a GCSE photography project, we're kind of in the right area and it doesn't look horrible". There was only so much we could do with that lighting – there was nothing we could bring in to tweak things. We knew we had to have a light at the front, but it wasn't powerful enough to bounce the light, to get more subtlety in the transitions between light and shade. And we were mostly at quite close range. Obviously the further away you are, the more softly the light hits the face. We took such a minimal kit. We could have taken more, but we didn't know enough about it.

Jack: Barry was a great way to kick things off. If we'd got someone a bit less outgoing… not that we needed to be encouraged to do the documentary, but it was encouraging for us to start the whole process with someone who was so friendly and so enthusiastic about the project.

Interviewing Barry McGuire in Frankfurt – where it really started.

With Barry McGuire and John & Sumi York, after a successful morning's work and before the long journey home.

GETTING IT TOGETHER PT.2

The approvals

Once we were home, we set about editing together a first draft of the New Christy Minstrels chapter of the film, using what we'd just shot, along with the archive clips and photos that we'd already been able to find. We sent it over to Gene's sons and their lawyer in the third week of June, then waited anxiously for a response. Finally, on July 5th, we got a one line message: "The response to the footage you sent was positive." A string of more expansive exchanges soon followed:

Date: Tue, 5 Jul 2011
Scott
I'm pleased to hear that. Essentially, plans are progressing on three fronts:
1) Putting together a schedule for our visit to the States in September to shoot interviews and location footage.
2) Tracking down and getting access to archive materials - mainly film footage and photos.
3) Negotiating preliminary licenses for those materials and for the recordings we intend to use.
We won't start editing in earnest until later in the year, when we've shot our original footage and have a clear idea of the archive materials available to us.
Paul

Date: Mon, 18 Jul 2011
Paul,
At this point I am interested in what interviews you have scheduled, and what resistance you have encountered, if any. Kai is willing to help you secure key interviews, so please do reach out to him. I think you have his cell phone number.
We are also interested in what recorded materials you plan to use. There are a lot of unreleased recordings floating around, many that

have been offered for release in the past and turned down by the family as not good representations of Gene Clark's work.
In general, having given the imprimatur to you and your project, Gene's sons want to make sure that you have the access you need and that you are using "A" list representations of Gene's work.
Scott

Monday, July 18, 2011 8:19 AM
Scott
I'm still working on an exact schedule for interviews, but up to this point, the following people have agreed to participate:
Roger McGuinn, Chris Hillman, Bernie Leadon, Doug Dillard, Michael Utley, Leland Sklar, Chip Douglas.
Chris Ethridge, Jerry Moss, Larry Marks, Ken Mansfield, Tom Slocum, Al Coury, Taj Mahal.
This is in addition to Barry McGuire and John York, who we've already done. I'm waiting to hear back from Tom Petty and Carla Olsen.
As I said in an earlier message, I'm hoping that Kai and Kelly will be able to make approaches to Carlie and Bonnie on our behalf or give us introductions.
I'm also hoping to speak with Philip Oleno in Mendocino and Jack Godden in Kansas City, but I'm waiting until we've got definite dates for being in those places before approaching them.
I also approached Sid Griffin, who said that, while he would be happy to give an interview, he didn't feel he could without your approval - perhaps you could let me know about that situation, so I can either go back to him or cross him off the list, as appropriate.
The one key person that we're having trouble getting to is David Crosby. I've been given Michael Jensen Communications as his management company, but I've not had any reply from them as yet.
If you have another line of approach into him, that would be very helpful.
As for the music, it's our intention to make maximum use of recordings that were issued during Gene's lifetime, with his approval. Our primary objective with this project has always been to make a contribution to increasing recognition of his music, particularly among people

who aren't overly familiar with it. I'm sure you'd agree that this will be best done by showcasing his best work - of which there is plenty for a documentary film - rather than previously unreleased material which, while of interest to hardcore fans and completists, won't really help our cause.

I've attached a preliminary list of titles that I'm asking my colleague, Chris France (who will be handling the licensing side of things), to look into. This list will no doubt expand/adapt as the project develops, but it should give you a clear indication of the kind of material we plan to use.

If there's anything else you'd like to know, please ask.

Paul

Date: Mon, 18 Jul 2011

Paul,

This is very helpful and I would like to speak with you this week about some of the entries. Kai is going to help you with the family interviews you want, and perhaps others. We want to make sure the focus is firmly fixed on Gene's music and life, and that the interviews are not hijacked by people with rusty axes to grind (or whatever) to rewrite history. Gene was a great talent and part of what we (me and Kelly and Kai), liked about you and your project is that it promised to focus on his great talent and not tabloid fare.

Scott

Not all of the interviewees mentioned in my message ended up being filmed, but several others came on board later in the process. Things had started to move forward quite quickly by this stage, with contacting people and researching potential travel arrangements. One of the big advantages of organising everything single-handed, was that I didn't need to wait for anyone else's go-ahead, now that we'd got the nod from Gene's sons. (There were also disadvantages, but they hadn't fully revealed themselves yet.)

Without further ado I started reaching out to the names on our interviewees list, making full use of the fact that we had the blessing of Gene's family. Meanwhile, I also sought to allay any concerns that they might continue to have.

Date: Mon, 18 Jul 2011
Scott
As I hope our original proposal makes clear, we want to make a film about Gene's life and music. The various issues and disagreements that have arisen since his death have no part in the story we intend to tell. And we have no more taste for tabloid-style sensationalism or muck raking than you do.
However, I hardly need to remind you that there was a darker side to Gene's life, as well as huge success and magnificent music. I'm not just talking about his problems with drink and drugs, but his ambivalent (sometimes, it seems, even self-destructive) attitude to that success, which hindered his talent in getting the recognition and rewards it deserved.
The focus of our film will be very much on Gene's music and songwriting, and what went into it. But that can't be done honestly by whitewashing. Like all great artists, his work was a product of the man he was and the life he led. There are indeed two sides to every story, not least this one, and we have to be allowed to reflect both of them.
I only met Gene once, but he struck me as a man with little taste for bullshit or dissembling. I think he would want his history to be told as accurately as possible, without rewriting for better or for worse. I'm sensitive to the fact that some of the people we hope to interview may, as you say, have rusty axes to grind. Equally, I've no doubt that others will prefer to view the past through rose-coloured glasses. Ultimately, we will have editorial control and will use that to avoid misrepresentation in either direction.
One last thing - we will have access to at least one video interview and a number of audio interviews with Gene. So hopefully a significant part of the story will come straight from the source.
Paul

Friday, July 22, 2011 11:53 AM
Scott
I haven't had a reply to my last message, so I'm just hoping I haven't put a cat among the pigeons. But I'd much rather be straight with you now than discover, further down the line, that we're not on the same wavelength.

I was watching a BBC documentary about Harry Nilsson earlier this week. 75 minutes long, of which the best part of 60 were spent dwelling on his wild living and long descent into alcoholism, career suicide and early death. His actual music was almost an irrelevance. That is absolutely NOT what we have in mind for our film.

By the same token, I saw recently saw another BBC production featuring Santana - a band I happen to know a lot about, having been a big fan from day one and spent some time on the road with them during my music journalist days. The title, 'Santana, Angels & Demons', suggested an honest appraisal of the tensions which both helped give the original band much of their creative edge and led to their break-up. In fact, it was anything but. Key issues in the Santana story were either glossed over or ignored and, while showcasing some great music, it was a disappointingly dull film. Again, NOT what we want to end up with.

I'm available most of next week to talk with yourself and/or Kai, as appropriate.

Meanwhile, have a good weekend.
Paul

Date: Fri, 22 Jul 2011 16:19:24 +0000
Paul,
I do not disagree with anything you said about truth telling. Of course, one can choose which truths to emphasize and that is where we would want to have a very open line of communication with you. It is the general intent and good faith of the producer (you), as much (maybe more) than the technical/ artistic quality of any proposed project which determines whether Gene Clark's sons are going to be supportive or not. We made certain judgements about where you were coming from, that resulted in your having Kelly and Kai Clark's

permission to tell others that they were supportive of your project. We did not think you had anything like the BBC doc on Nilsson in mind, and if we had thought that, the Clarks would not have been supportive. Nor did we expect to have prior approval over your work -- we are not commissioning you to do a vanity piece. However, we want to make sure that communications are very open because we know from many years of experience dealing with Gene Clark's friends and hangers on, that some would like to change history or their place in it. Your statement that "the issues and disagreements that have arisen since his death have no part in the story" resolves most of the concerns I have.
Scott

Fri 22/07/2011
Scott
I'm very glad to hear that.
You have my absolute assurance regarding good faith and good intent. I'm doing this because I love Gene's music and think it deserves greater recognition. (As it happens, from the short time I spent with him, I also liked the man. But that's secondary.)
On the artistic/technical side of things, I believe we have the skills and resources to make a film that's worthy of Gene's memory, and we will be doing (are doing) everything we can to achieve that.
As for open lines of communication, we seem to have that already and I see no reason why it should change. In fact, I hope they will get stronger, particularly once we come to California and have an opportunity to meet with Kelly and Kai.
Many thanks
Paul

The arrangements

We'd identified September as the ideal time to go to America for the main shoot. Doing it earlier would have taken us into the school summer holiday period, with higher travel costs and possibly less availability for any interviewees planning to go away with children or grandchildren. Any later and the chances of getting unfavourable weather conditions would start to increase. Tricia and I already had a trip to Kefalonia booked for the first week of September and I wasn't about to test her sympathy for the project by cancelling that, so we penciled in the rest of the month into early October, with more precise details to depend on when and where we could set up interviews.

The original hope was to start in Los Angeles before going north to San Francisco and Mendocino, then across to Kansas City en route for home. As things turned out, we had to make two separate visits to LA, to accommodate all the interviewees in that area. Which put extra miles on the clock, but at least made things much simpler in terms of returning the Californian hire car and lighting rig. And Mr (or rather Mrs) McGuinn's reluctance to meet us anywhere but close to their home meant we had to stop off in Orlando between Kansas City and journey's end.

Constructing an itinerary that worked around the availability of the people we most wanted to get on film, while not involving ridiculous amounts of travelling hither and thither, took some doing. But eventually we had enough in place to book our plane flights, intercontinental and internal, with a reasonable degree of confidence. We would be spending two weeks in California and five days in Kansas/Missouri, before our final stop off in Florida. We expected there to be some changes of plan within that (and there were). We just had to trust that they wouldn't be too disruptive or damaging.

As August went by, and more interviews started falling into place, I was also booking all the other things we'd be needing – hotel rooms, hire cars and the buying or hiring of equipment, from cameras and lights to DV tapes and hard drives. By the time Tricia and I went off to the Ionian Sea for a much-needed break, we were as ready as we'd ever be. Which was just as well… we'd be getting back from Greece on the Thursday evening and flying out to LA on the Sunday morning. There was just time to wash clothes and repack, and organize baggage with Jack and Dan, to make sure we'd got everything and had distributed it so that none of the cases were exceeding weight limits and incurring extra charges.

THE AMERICAN SHOOT

Jack - By the time we got out there, I knew the main thing was going to be the interviews. And I knew from when we did Barry Maguire and John York that they were alright, because once we got the lighting set up it was just a locked off camera and a roaming one. And I knew we could do that alright. We didn't know about the locations. But I also knew that, with the locations, because it was basically going to be locked off shots, it was just about the camera settings and where the sun was going to be. Again, that was Daniel's department and he was fine with that. He wasn't out of his element. He was able to say "These are the settings and the sun's over there, so let's have it angled this way". Once we got out of LA, the pressure was definitely off, because then it was just daytime location shots and interviews. It was only when we were in LA and matching what was there to what I had in my head – the Entourage opening and the driving lights and the neon, and I wanted to get the classic 'looking up at the palm trees as they go past'.

Day 1 – 11/09/2011 – London to Los Angeles

Jack - All I remember about flying out to LA was looking to see what films were on. They had 'Senna', which I was excited about because I wanted to see it, and watching that got me in the mood for our shoot, because that was another tragic story of a famous person who burned brightly and died tragically. A completely different style of documentary, but the mood and tone of it I remember thinking "That's what I want to capture".

As we sat in the departure lounge at Heathrow, Jack voiced his opinion that LHR>LAX was "the king of flights". This was based on his obsession with movies and the people involved in their making, and his ambition to eventually 'go Hollywood' as a director and/or screenwriter. He was hoping we'd be sharing the flight with some A, or at least B listers. I was happy to be giving him his first, though hopefully not last experience of that flight, but suggested that any such luminaries would be chilling in the first-class lounge and enjoying a section of the plane that was completely segregated from our economy class seats. Which, of course, turned out to be the case.

Jack - If we were on the plane to LA now, I'd be thinking "I haven't done enough research. I don't know which shots to get there. We could do this or that." If we were doing it now, I'd do more research on Gene Clark himself. Being out in America doing the interviews was like putting together a jigsaw puzzle… this is the narrative and this is how it will piece together. If it was this year, I would read the books and so on. But I didn't. I don't know why. I'm sure it wasn't a deliberate decision. But I'd be worried now that, if I didn't do the research, I'd be missing out on things we could have done. Something narratively clever I could have done, with the shots we got. That kind of pre-planning worked with Barry McGuire, because I saw the archive footage before and was able to go "Oh, we could do this transition to that". Probably I was shutting it off, because if I had read it all up it might have been too much and I'd have panicked. It might have been better, in the end, that we did just take it day by day. I think I would have been too professionally immature, at that point, to have taken it well. I think I would have panicked too much and worried about it too much. But in the end it worked out alright.

We got into LA by mid-afternoon local time and whisked through the arrivals hall, completely avoiding the hassles around carnets and customs clearance and work permits, that a normal film crew would have to engage with. So far as officialdom was concerned, we were just a family group of photography enthusiasts on holiday. Our passports were stamped and we were sent on our way with a cheery "Happy trails".

After picking up a capacious station wagon at a ridiculously low price, by European standards, we stopped off at a branch of Radio Shack to buy a cheap cellphone (using our UK mobiles in the States would have been way more expensive) and headed to our hotel close to Sunset Boulevard. Dan and Jack went to check out the lie of the land and be unsuccessfully propositioned by a couple of gentlemen with an eye for young flesh, while I made the first important connection of the trip. The guy with the lighting rig brought it to the hotel, exactly as promised, and we elected to lug it up to the room, rather than taking the risk of leaving it in the car overnight.

When Dan and Jack returned from their recce, we strolled up to the Strip to take in iconic landmarks such as The Whisky A Go Go and The Viper Room, before seeking out The Rainbow Bar & Grill for sustenance. The Strip has long since lost its status as the launch pad for new talent and many of the venues frequented by the great names in music and movies in earlier decades have been replaced by office blocks, apartment buildings and parking lots. Those that remain have become tourist attractions and the real scene has moved out to other parts of the city. But it was still a thrill to be following in so many famous footsteps and I took great pleasure in explaining to Dan and Jack why they should also be feeling privileged to find themselves on hallowed ground.

While eating we discussed our plan of attack for the coming weeks. We had a full schedule of interviews – at least 24, spread over the length of California and the width of the country, with the possibility of more to be added – but I also wanted to get as much footage as possible of the places where Gene had lived and worked. B roll as it used to be known, in the old days when material was captured on film rather than memory cards. We wouldn't be getting much time for sightseeing and relaxation, and we would have to be ready to improvise. We'd be learning to use the largely unfamiliar equipment as we went along and precise details of locations would only be revealed when we arrived at them. Location scouting was just one of many industry norms that our minimal budget and resources didn't stretch to.

We went to bed, in our now cluttered hotel room, already feeling knackered after a very long day. Which was probably just as well, otherwise feelings of anticipation and nervousness would probably have got in the way of a much-needed good night's sleep.

Jack - I remember when we arrived in LA and got to our hotel, going through the lobby, there was a massive group of young kids, who I assumed were on a school trip or something, talking with what I assumed was a teacher. Then later that evening, when we turned on the TV in our room, it was 'America's Got Talent' and the kids we'd seen downstairs in the lobby were getting kicked off and the person they'd been speaking to was their coach or something. I thought that was an interesting reminder of the fleeting nature of fame, as we were about to start making this documentary about Gene Clark. That these kids had come to LA from wherever, been on TV and were now heading back to oblivion.

Day 2 – 12/09/2011 – Los Angeles

Our first day of shooting threw us in at the deep end, practically and emotionally, as we interviewed Carla Olson, Saul Davis and Pat Robinson.

We met them at Saul's brother's house on the outskirts of town. It was a reasonably large place, which offered a variety of settings (an important consideration, as we wanted each of the three interviews to have its own look) and the tranquillity of a suburban side street (another important consideration, as any significant amount of ambient noise would have made sound recording tricky). Considering we'd had no say in choosing it and no idea what we would be getting, we were relieved.

Jack - I didn't know who was important and who was less important. Obviously we wanted to get them all, but to me Carla Olson was the same as Mike Utley. I didn't know who was going to be a main part of the story and who wasn't. I didn't know who was "Oh, we'll only need a few moments out of them in the final edit" or who was a lynchpin and if we don't get good stuff out of them, then the whole thing kind of falls apart. So I wasn't more nervous or less nervous for any of the interviews. We just kind of went along. My main thing was that I knew we just had to go in and, within 40 mins or so, me and Dan had to have recced the place and set up the lights.

Dan and Jack needed a while to find the best spots for filming the three interviews and to familiarise themselves with the lighting gear they were unpacking, which gave me time to have a stab at establishing a rapport with our three subjects.

It had taken some work to get to this point with Saul – and therefore with Carla. When I first made contact with potential interviewees, it immediately became clear that there were issues between Saul and the estate. Most seemingly related to the handling of Gene's legacy, particularly recordings that he'd left in his wake. I'd been forewarned about this by Johnny Rogan, who had spoken extensively with everyone involved, when researching his books about The Byrds. But even so, I was surprised at what seemed to be the extent of the ill feeling.

When I emailed him in early May, Saul initially said that he and Carla would want no part in what we were doing and, even more regrettably, that he could put a spanner in the works with other people on our wish list, who he knew.

Then Sid Griffin indicated that his involvement might potentially upset both Saul and the estate, so it might be best if he didn't get involved. For a while, it looked as if we would have to make some difficult choices about who we were able to end up having in the film.

Lucky Break #5

Soon after these ill-omened exchanges with Saul and Sid, we did the first shoot with Barry McGuire and John York in Germany. Unknown to us, John then gave glowing reports about us and our approach to

the project, both to Saul and to Gene's sons, back in the States.
Unknown to him, this turned out to be instrumental in getting those
parties onside. Relationships warmed significantly, on all fronts, from
then on and all of the above gave us whole-hearted co-operation in
various ways. If you ever read this, John... we're eternally grateful.

Nevertheless, given the delicate negotiations that had brought us to this
point, I wanted to do everything possible to create an amicable
atmosphere, in which all three of our interviewees would feel
comfortable and willing to open up.

As I'd expected, Saul did most of the talking while we waited to start
the interviews, bigging up the closeness to Gene of their musical and
social circle and their importance in his story. The truth was, they'd
only got involved in the last few years of Gene's life and at a very low
point in it. But Carla had done some fine work with him and the story of
those final years needed to be told, so I wasn't about to question his
viewpoints or assertations.

We put Saul in the main room of the house, with a large poster of
traditional Spanish dancers behind him. For some reason this had put
Jack in mind of 'Citizen Kane' and business moguldom... a bit of a
stretch, in Saul's case, but it made an interesting setting and I was
happy to go along with it. Carla sat on the veranda, accompanied by a
Stars & Stripes flag wafting in the breeze, which felt right for the
traditionally inflected music (later to be known as 'Americana'), which
she and Gene had made together. Pat, looking more like a WWE
wrestler than a musician, ended up in front of some anonymous louvre
doors. Not the most compelling of set ups, but he had a screen presence
which compensated for its blandness.

Jack – They look like three completely different locations. That's what I
like about that. Saul looks like he's in some kind of gothic mansion.
Carla looks like she might be on a farm in some rural location. Pat is in

a more domestic situation. But actually all three of them were within five yards of each other.

Dan - Lighting the ones outside were tricky, because there was moving light and in LA, when the sun hits you it's so different to being in the shade. Also we didn't have any neutral density filters for the cameras. With a film camera you'd shoot at low shutter speeds, so if it's really bright light you have to open up to a massive aperture – which our shots weren't, there'd be too much in focus in layman's terms. Our shoots inside were the opposite. We were trying to get a very narrow, shallow depth of field.

All three gave us really good, heartfelt interviews and we left feeling we'd got off to an excellent start, after all the stresses and concerns.

Jack - On that first day, with Saul, Carla and Pat, the pressure was off a bit. We didn't have to be in and out and off to another place within a certain time. I remember them being very friendly, so that was a good way to open it. It seemed quite relaxed.

On the way back into town, we stopped off to shoot some footage of The Troubadour club and Dan Tana's restaurant, next door to each other on Santa Monica Boulevard. Both notable LA landmarks and both of them, we were delighted to find, looking much as they had done back in the day.

The Troubadour was where Gene Clark and Roger McGuinn first got together, forming what would become The Beefeaters, then The Jet Set and ultimately The Byrds, and it was the focal point for the singer/songwriter boom during the late '60s and early '70s, as a place to play and a place to meet. A long list of celebrated names, from Elton John to (The) Eagles, got their start within its walls. For once, the much over-used term 'legendary' is appropriate. Gene played several showcase gigs there over the years, with different combos, each of which he managed to sabotage with bizarre behaviour and/or by being in an altered state.

Dan Tana's was (and continued to be, until the pandemic interrupted things) a favourite eaterie and watering hole among the Hollywood elite. It has a notorious part in Gene's story, as the setting for an alleged attempted assault on David Geffen, following the failure of the 'No Other' album on Geffen's Asylum label. Accounts of this incident – and the damage it did to Gene's future prospects – differ in details. We'd hoped to get a horse's mouth account from Mr Geffen himself, but all our efforts to contact him went unanswered. Perhaps not surprisingly. It's unlikely to be the moment in his staggeringly successful career that he's most eager to revisit. In fact he's denied it ever happened, although there are many others citing first or second-hand evidence that it did.

Shooting on a busy LA street quickly brought home the advantages of travelling very light, in both personnel and equipment. To anyone looking on, we would have looked like tourists taking souvenir snaps, rather than a film crew in need of appropriate authorisation and permits. Over the next three weeks, we would pick up location footage in a wide variety of settings. Only once did anyone ever challenge us about what we were doing.

Now we knew how easy it was to shoot in public places, and as The Troubadour and Dan Tana's were only a short walk from our hotel, we went back later to get them again at night.

Day 3 – 13/09 – Los Angeles/Pasadena

Somewhat refreshed as jet lag wore off and instilled with optimism, after a good start to our work, we set off on a day of two halves – an interview in the morning and some serious location work thereafter.

The interview was one I was particularly looking forward to. As an aspiring bass player, one of my role models was and is Leland Sklar, otherwise known as Lee. Not the most famous bassist in the world but a man with a fantastic CV, stretching all the way back to the late '60s. He's worked with everyone from James Taylor and Jackson Browne to Phil Collins and Leonard Cohen. If you haven't got an album with him on it, you probably need to reassess your collection. His contributions to Gene's 'No Other' album are nothing short of majestic.

We went to his home on the outskirts of Pasadena, which at first sight looked like a house that had stood for centuries in the heart of the English countryside. It was, of course, far more contemporary than that, and was more a tribute to American architects' talent for pastiche than a piece of history.

While the outside was beautiful, the inside was extraordinary. Lee told us that, during his years of touring the world, he'd chosen to spend his off-duty hours scouring local shops and markets for souvenirs, rather than engaging in more traditional rock'n'roll pastimes. As a result, the house was full of everything from strange musical instruments to exotic ornaments. It was like walking into a museum or exhibition gallery. His collection of Father Christmas figures alone was worth the price of admission. The problem, for filming, was finding a room with space to set up the lights without major reorganisation and a background that wasn't so busy that it might distract from the interviewee – even one as eye-catching as the spectacularly bearded Mr Sklar.

Dan - He had a weird house. In his toilet – and I don't understand why – he had this image that was like a collage of photos and illustrations of The Two Fat Ladies, who hosted food programmes on TV. They were the female equivalents of The Two Hairy Bikers. I asked Jack to go to have a look, and he confirmed that it was The Two Fat Ladies. But it would have been even weirder, I guess, if it was just a stand-alone portrait of them.

We eventually decided to shoot outside, under a tree in the garden, close enough to the house to run extension cables for the lights. In case you were wondering, we needed them even in bright daylight, to attempt a consistency of look as the sun moved round while we were filming. There was minimal breeze and ambient noise, apart from a short spell when one of the neighbours started mowing their lawn, so everything went smoothly and Lee gave us a supremely articulate, entertaining interview. He had clear and fond memories of working with Gene, and also offered an enlightening insight into the very different world of recording in the pre-digital age.

Jack - Lee Sklar had this crazy house… a nice house, but sometimes you had to think about what would capture the person and the mood we wanted to create. If we'd shot Lee Sklar in his crazy Christmas room or Halloween room with loads of horror stuff, that would have looked more interesting than what we actually shot, but it would have been so distracting and weird. Then one of his neighbours started mowing the lawn, within the first ten minutes, and we just had to fight through it. Again, my naivety was a bit of a benefit. If that was now, I'd say "We need to shut off this interview and move somewhere else" and that would have taken up more time. Whereas at the time I thought we might not hear it and in the end we didn't, which was fine. But if it was now, I'd be thinking "We'll definitely hear that".

Dan – Leland was a nice guy. He seemed the one that most had his head screwed on. He had a happy memory of working with Gene and seemed like a man who enjoyed that part of his life and was still enjoying his life. For whatever reason… I guess he didn't drink or do as many drugs as some others. He clearly had a talent as well and he was obviously passionate, which I liked. After one of the No Other sessions – and he's basically a session musician, so he just gets paid for the session – he went back in and did some overdubs, which make the album more of a sonic thing than it would have been otherwise. He felt like a man who, if he was going to do something, wanted to do it the best he could.

Our next stop was also in Pasadena, to meet with a chap who was going to show us around the Laurel Canyon area, where Gene had lived during the sixties, along with most of LA's musical community of the time. Domenic Priore is a noted author and broadcaster, who probably knows more about the history of that scene than anyone else alive. We couldn't have had a better guide.

But first we had to find him. In the days before everyone had Google Maps on their phone, we were relying on his directions. A good hour of driving round ensued, exchanging increasingly frustrated phone calls, before we were finally able to hook up. But it was well worth the hassle. Laurel Canyon Boulevard, which winds down through the hills from Mulholland Drive to Sunset Boulevard, past the landmark Country Store, is easy enough to get to. Running off either side of the main drag, however, is a tangle of increasingly narrow and twisty streets (what we'd call 'lanes' in England), which is where Gene and his assorted compadres had their residences. If we'd been looking for them unaided, we'd probably still be trying to get out of the maze.

Filming there wasn't easy, partly because some of the houses were hidden away behind screens of foliage and partly because there was almost nowhere to park the car. Mostly I had to stay with it, to move on if necessary, while Jack and Dan hopped out with Domenic to show them what was what. Once again, having very portable and unobtrusive equipment was a bonus. Especially when we went to shoot the Country Store. Domenic was concerned that we'd get into trouble, as the store's owners were apparently very protective of their image rights and would expect to charge a location fee, if they knew we were making a film. But since we were indistinguishable from anyone else getting their souvenir snaps, we passed unnoticed.

From the Canyon, we went along Mulholland to a viewpoint overlooking the Hollywood Bowl amphitheatre and the great spread of Los Angeles, stretching out as far as the eye could see, down to the ocean. From here we set up a camera to shoot on time lapse, to capture the dying of the light over the city. This would be part of a planned sequence in the film, covering Gene's relocation from the hurly burly of LA to the tranquillity of Northern California.

When we finally lost the light, we headed back down to the Strip to drive along it a few times, shooting through an open window, getting the crowded sidewalks and neon and signage for the same sequence.

By the time this was done it was quite late in the evening and we were starving, so we rewarded ourselves with dinner at Mel's Drive-In back on Sunset. Not the Mel's immortalised in 'American Graffitti', sadly. That was in San Francisco and was demolished years ago. But this one occupies the building that was once Ben Franks, the coffee shop that was a favourite post-gig hangout for bands playing at The Whisky and other venues in the area. While we stuffed ourselves with classic burgers in classic diner surroundings, Domenic filled Jack and Dan in with further details of why they were in a very special place.

After dinner, en route to taking Domenic home, we shot some footage of the Strip at night, in all its neon glory, with endless traffic streaming along it.

Jack - The main reference for the LA stuff was the opening credits of 'Entourage', where they had quick flashes of the signs up and down Sunset Strip. I wanted to try and emulate that. But with the 5D we weren't able to do that very well. We only ended up using it in small snippets, so I was able to cherry pick the best bits. And we'd gone up and down the Strip so many times that there was loads of it, so in the end it didn't look too bad. But I wouldn't have been able to use it much more than we did.
Looking back I wish I'd done the research. I thought that you just ran the camera and sped it up in the edit. But actually that's not how you do it. You have to do it in stills. You take a still every 10 seconds or 30 seconds or whatever and edit them together. I don't know if Dan knew

that. Maybe I just hadn't communicated to him that we'd be doing time lapse. My idea in LA was to get time lapse of traffic flowing past the camera, so there'd be these streams of light. Had we done the time lapse the correct way, with the stills, that would have come across quite nicely. But we didn't do that. The time lapse of the sunset we were able to use and that did look good, because it was during the day. But the traffic was at night. It just looked really grainy and rubbish.

Day 4 – 14/09 – Los Angeles to Ventura

Our first port of call, as we moved on from LA, was to be Ventura, about sixty miles further up the coast. We were due to arrive at Chris Hillman's home at 11 o'clock and we didn't want to be late. No-one had a more consistent association with Gene throughout his musical career, from being flatmates at the birth of The Byrds to playing on almost all his albums after leaving the group. It was an interview that would be essential to the film and needed to be good. Chris had a reputation for being a man who doesn't like being messed about, however, so we set off in plenty of time to arrive ahead of schedule.

Unfortunately, as things turned out, Ventura wasn't our first port of call. That was Oxnard, a sprawling town with a large commercial harbour, a naval base, industrial estates and business parks, and a tangle of roads connecting them. We had to go through Oxnard, at a snail's pace, because Route 101 – the main highway heading north from LA along the Pacific coast – was closed due to an accident. We managed to arrive at our destination only 15 minutes behind our expected arrival, but we could tell Chris wasn't impressed.

Thankfully he and his wife are strong on family, and it was equally obvious they were quite taken with the fact that I was undertaking this project with two of my sons. It emerged that we'd also been given a positive reference by Gene's son Kai, who Chris knows well. Leaving nothing to chance, while Jack and Dan set up to shoot on the patio, I made a point of establishing that I was fully aware of his own musical history, which includes membership of The Byrds, The Flying Burrito Brothers and Manassas with Stephen Stills, as well as leading his own bands. So, by the time we sat down to start the interview, I think it's fair to say we were getting on famously.

As a result, the hour that Chris had originally granted us stretched to two, as he reminisced and theorised at length about his relationship and work with Gene. He's a very experienced interviewee, which I knew has the potential to produce something that's either a bit cagey or delivered by rote, or both. But what he gave us felt spontaneous, honest and engaged. It was everything I'd hoped for and more, and we left knowing that a central plank of our film was now in place.

Jack - At the end of the interview, while we were packing away, Chris started talking about the day Gene died. He was saying about how Saul had phoned him and he had to calm Saul down, and I wished we'd got that on camera. In the end we got enough stuff from everyone else and didn't need that, but I remember thinking "Oh God, we've just lost a gem. Now we haven't got that in the edit, we're not going to get anything as good as that again." But we did. You'd asked Saul and Carla, so maybe you were only going to ask people who you thought were involved with Gene at that stage. But I said we needed to ask everyone, just in case they came up with something good.

From Ventura we turned inland, to the hillside residence of Larry Marks, who had produced both Dillard & Clark albums and become a friend of Gene's during his post-Byrds period in LA. Larry was in very poor physical health (he passed away in early 2013) and we were shown into the house by his carer. But there was nothing wrong with his mental faculties.

Despite the excesses that he and Gene shared, he had clear recollections of their time together and it was great to get a first-hand account of how Dillard & Clark were formed and then fell apart. As a staff producer at Columbia Records during the mid '60s, he'd also had a front row seat for the meteoric rise of The Byrds, and it was interesting to be given an independent view of their impact on the music scene.

With six interviews and some decent location footage already in the bag, we were starting to feel that all the planning and preparation was paying off.

<u>Day 5 – 15/09 – Ventura to Santa Barbara, via Los Angeles</u>

The day started with nipping back to LA, to meet keyboard player Michael Utley at his home in the Venice area of LA. Not perfect route planning, but it was the only connection we could make between our itinerary and his busy schedule of recording and touring.

Despite his lengthy career at an elite level of the music business (he has well over four hundred credits on the Discogs website alone), I got the feeling that Michael wasn't the most experienced of interviewees. Combine that with the fact that he's a very sweet man, who clearly didn't want to say anything that might upset anyone, and we got one of our more restrained interviews, despite my best efforts to draw him out. He'd worked with Gene and Jesse Ed Davis, and then with Gene and Tommy Kaye – two hell-raising duos, by all accounts – so he must have witnessed something worth the telling. His motto was obviously "what happens in the studio stays in the studio", however, and he wasn't about to spill any beans. But he had some good input on Gene as a songwriter - what made his songs distinctive and what it was like to work with the material he gave to his musicians.

On the way back out of LA, we stopped off at Village Recorders, the studio where Gene had made a couple of his finest albums. We spent a few minutes shooting the exterior and were about to head off, when the door burst open and a man came out, demanding to know what we were doing. We'd been caught by the CCTV cameras around the building and suspicions had been raised. Presumably they didn't expect tourists to be taking multiple happy snaps of their establishment. Our interrogator was the studio manager and once we'd explained what we were doing, his manner changed completely. He invited us inside, showed us the rooms where Gene's recordings had taken place and sent us on our way with offers of further assistance, if any were needed.

Then it was off to Santa Barbara, a two hour cruise up the 101 (now thankfully clear again), where we were meeting Tom Slocum, one of Gene's closest friends in the last two decades of his life. Talking with Tom couldn't have been more different to our earlier experience with Michael Utley. From the moment we arrived, before we'd even set up to start shooting, he delivered a non-stop stream of recollections, anecdotes, psychoanalysis and speculation, which went on for well over two hours. By the time we departed, we were elated but exhausted.

Dan - Tom Slocum was a bit wacky. I quite liked him. If there was a film about his life, David Walliams could have played him. Or Frankie Howerd would have been perfect.

Jack and Dan had plans for the evening, meeting up with a friend who lived in Santa Barbara. But before that, as soon as we checked in to our motel for the night, Jack started his daily task of uploading that day's footage onto a hard drive. Which should have been routine, but on this occasion led to a bit of panic, as the Michael Utley interview couldn't be found. Had that memory card been mislaid or corrupted or recorded over or accidentally wiped? This was stuff beyond my very limited technical knowledge, so I left him and Dan to it, while I went looking for a beer. By the time I returned the problem had been resolved. That particular card had been found and everyone could relax.

I dropped the boys off at their friend's house, then went back to have a much-needed early night. Next day I'd be driving us up to San Francisco, a journey of just over 300 miles. Which usually would only take a few hours and be no big deal, especially on American freeways. But I wanted to take State Route 1, the fabled Pacific Coast Highway, which would be much slower, especially as it wound along the Big Sur stretch of the coast. This would show us some magnificent scenery and take us in the footsteps of some notable American characters, such as Jack Kerouac and Hunter S. Thompson. A roster which includes Gene Clark himself, as he ventured out of LA in search of an escape from the rigours and temptations of the music business. We were hopeful it would give us some more location shots that we could use in that chapter of his story.

Day 6 – 16/09 – Santa Barbara to San Francisco

I had a sound, undisturbed sleep and when I woke up, just after eight o'clock the next morning, I realised why. Dan and Jack hadn't come back. Not wanting to delay setting off on our longish journey up to San Francisco, I immediately tried to ring them. Several attempts went unanswered so I decided to head to their friend's house, crossing my fingers that they would be there, rather than sleeping it off in a shop doorway or taking up space in the local police station.

At this point, I should say that the friend's 'house' was actually a mansion – a proper mansion (albeit an American style one) set in several acres of grounds. His father had started the Kinko chain of copy shops and sold it for hundreds of millions of dollars a few years earlier. A fact which was never mentioned in publicity or interviews about the friend's band, who presented themselves as authentic New York punks from the dark end of the street. I had to wait at the ornamental gates for some while, periodically ringing the entrance bell, before a half-awake voice finally responded. I don't know what time the lads' night out had concluded, but as soon as I set eyes on Dan and Jack I was grateful that they wouldn't be expected to do much for the next few hours, other than avoid throwing up in the car (a task which Jack only just managed to accomplish).

Jack - That was our one experience of drink and debauchery on that trip. I wasn't even sure I wanted to do it, because I was just so stressed out about the rest of the trip, but Dan persuaded me. So we went to this guy's house, which was a proper '60s style mansion. We spent a lot of the evening sitting out by the pool drinking and from there we went out to some bar, and then we ended up getting a lift from there back to the house. Even though I was drunk, I remember on that car ride saying I was going to have to throw up, and while the car was driving I opened the door and threw up. But at least I threw up out of the car. My next memory is that you were picking us up the next morning. But the reason I threw up on the way to San Francisco was that, in the car, I was having to sort out transferring stuff with my laptop on my lap on these windy roads, when I was feeling hungover anyway.

We made some stops along the way, including a rocky beach with an impressive colony of elephant seals and Hearst Castle at San Simeon, the lavish creation of media tycoon William Randolph Hearst. Jack, being an avid student of movie history, did at least come alive for that bit, as the Castle was the template for Citizen Kane's Xanadu.

Having set off later than planned, we hit San Francisco in perfect time for the evening rush hour. A couple of near misses ensued, as we negotiated unfamiliar and overcrowded streets in search of our motel. We got there unscathed, however, just as darkness was falling and Jack promptly retired to bed, to complete his recovery from the previous night's exploits, while Dan and I went to meet Gene's elder son, Kelly.

This was a significant rendezvous. Kelly was far more reserved than his younger brother, Kai, and generally kept a low profile. Although we'd had a couple of email exchanges, he was still very unsure about sitting in front of a camera to talk about his father, and we only had this one opportunity to convince him that it would be a good thing to do.

Lucky Break #6

We hooked up with Kelly at a bar close to our hotel. After a few minutes of somewhat awkward introductory chat I was starting to wonder how the conversation could be moved in a more productive

*direction, without scaring him off. Then we took our drinks outside,
so Dan and I could have a smoke. Dan offered Kelly a cigarette,
which he declined in favour of chewing on a toothpick. He told us he
was trying to give up, after returning from a backpacking trip round
South America. Dan had been on a very similar adventure the
previous year, so the two of them started swapping travellers' tales. By
the time they finished, the ice was thoroughly broken and Kelly raised
the subject of arrangements for the interview, with no need for
persuasion.*

*Dan - I don't want to take any credit for that. By the time we had the
meeting he wasn't going to be like "Fuck you guys, I'm not doing it". I
think it was more "They've come all the way to San Francisco. They
seem nice enough. Let's just do it." He just wasn't that interested in it, I
think, in terms of talking about his Dad. I don't think it was on his
radar to be that interested in doing it. It took us going to San Francisco
and arranging to meet up. I don't think there was going to be a point,
unless we were really intense dickheads, that he was going to say "I'm
not getting involved in that". By the time we were there and we met him
in the evening, he must have thought "These guys seem alright". I
think it would have taken a lot, at that point, for him to say "Fuck, I'm
not doing it". I just think he was a bit blasé about it. He wasn't super
hyped about doing it.*

Day 7 – 17/09 – San Francisco to Mendocino

In my brief email exchanges with Kelly he'd suggested the possibility
of doing the interview in the so-called 'poster room' at the Fillmore, the
fabled venue for numerous extraordinary gigs over the years, where he
did occasional work. To the best of my knowledge, Gene had never
played there, but I was excited by the prospect of seeing the place and
filming in it.

As it turned out, it wasn't available on the one morning we were able to
shoot Kelly, so we went to his house instead. He had a fully equipped

motorcycle workshop in the basement, which worked perfectly as a location. It was an ideal backdrop for him and being on home turf clearly helped him feel reasonably relaxed about the situation. After all the uncertainty, he gave us a great interview. He seemed more intent on telling his truth than airbrushing his dad's legacy, and it felt like he was unburdening himself of a load he'd been carrying for years. We spent longer than expected with him, so we had to pack up in a hurry, to avoid being overly delayed getting to our next appointment.

Jack - We looked around Kelly's house, trying to figure out where to shoot the interview with him, and I remember it was quite cramped – one of those old San Francisco town houses. And we were asking if there was anywhere else and eventually he said "Well, there's my garage". That had loads of bike stuff in it and we thought that was perfect. I don't know why he hadn't shown us that anyway. Maybe he thought we wanted something a bit more formal.

Dan – I think he gave us one of the very best interviews. I remember me and Jack looking at each other at points and thinking he was wearing his heart on his sleeve. The bit at the end, where he said he wished his Dad had been a carpenter or something, and not a famous man. It felt like he was unloading.

Jack – He actually had a way with words. He was quite poetic, although he probably didn't realise it. Like his father. An instinctive feel for words was probably in his DNA.

With Kelly successfully done and dusted, we left San Francisco and drove north east across the Bay (or, more accurately, the bays) to Vacaville, where Peter Oliva awaited us. Peter had been part of the Mendocino fraternity in the mid '70s and played bass in Gene's KC Southern Band – the group he'd brought over to the UK when I met him in 1977. Like many of his generation, Peter had found Jesus, given up his wild ways and was now living about sixty miles from San Francisco in the Sacramento Valley. Once we'd got clear of the city we made good time and arrived only a few minutes late.

Unlike Chris Hillman, Peter wasn't in the least concerned by our lack of precise punctuality and his interview was yet another marked contrast to the one we'd done in the morning. A big guy with a ready laugh, he was a born raconteur and was eager to share his tales – some funny, some bittersweet – of the time he'd spent making music and raising a ruckus with Gene. It was with regret that we had to turn down his invitation to stay for a barbecue, as we had another long drive ahead of us.

Our destination that evening, and our base for the next couple of days, was the much anticipated (at least, by me) Mendocino. A cross-country drive of at least five hours from Vacaville, which we ideally wanted to complete before nightfall. It was actually a glorious trip, across the Napa Valley with its endless vineyards, then up through miles of mighty forests towards the coast, breathing in the heady aroma of countless redwood trees. We finally emerged from the woods to find ourselves looking directly onto the Pacific Ocean and the start of a spectacular sunset. We immediately pulled over, got the cameras out and spent the next half hour capturing it.

By the time we completed the journey to Mendocino, darkness had descended completely. After keeping accommodation costs to a minimum thus far, I'd decided to allow the budget to treat us to a modest step up in comfort and we checked into the well-reviewed Little River Inn, just outside Mendocino overlooking the sea. We felt we'd earned it. And we were able to persuade ourselves it had some relevance to our story. Gene had made several visits to Little River, when he first discovered this part of the country, and had written songs for the 'Roadmaster' and 'White Light' albums in a small cabin that he rented, just a stone's throw from where we were now staying.

Day 8 – 18/09 – Mendocino

Much as we'd have liked a lie-in, we had an early start and a full day
ahead of us. Kai, Gene's younger son, came to meet us and was our
guide to the right people and the right places. Kai, himself a musician
and performer, was much more outgoing than his brother and we soon
established an easy rapport. Knowing how important Mendocino had
been to his father's life and work, we told him we wanted to capture as
much of its surroundings and atmosphere as possible, as well as doing
the interviews we had scheduled.

First stop was the 19th century stagecoach house, surrounded by
redwoods, which Gene had bought when he and Carlie got married. It
had played host to some of the happiest times of his life and some of the
most desolate, after the marriage broke down. It was now owned by an
elderly couple who knew Kai and were happy to let us spend as long as
we liked, wandering around the property and getting it on film.

Then on to another house, buried deep in the woods, where we met
Philip Oleno. Philip and his wife Ea had been Gene and Carlie's closest
friends, during the golden days of their time in Mendocino. Ea had
passed away in 2008, which had hit Philip very hard. Kai had warned us
that he was still not in a good place and probably wouldn't want to
appear on camera. He welcomed us into his home, however, and
seemed pleased to see Kai.

We chatted for a while, not wishing to rush things, and he started asking
questions about our project. He'd been a student at the UCLA film
school, where his roommate had been one James Douglas Morrison,
before heading north to become a woodworker and metalsmith, so he
had an informed interest. This led on quite easily to my asking
questions about his and Ea's relationship with Gene and Carlie. Dan
and Jack unobtrusively set up the lights and cameras while we talked
and, without making a big deal of it, we ended up shooting a series of
intimate, first-hand recollections.

Jack - That was one of those things, like David Crosby, where the slowness of Philip speaking didn't seem wrong. It came across alright. I don't know if you were worried about it when you were interviewing him, but he just seemed thoughtful and reflective rather than slow and ponderous. We had lots of different kinds of energy from different people. When we got there, I thought we were just going to be shooting around another place where Gene used to hang out. I didn't know some shambling old cabin man was going to come out. I remember this mysterious figure coming to the door and giving us the blessing to come into his cabin. And when we went in, you gave me and Dan a heads up to just be sensible... not do anything that might upset him or put him off. So we went in, really reverential and I was expecting something out of Deadwood, but he had a bunch of Sopranos boxsets, which surprised me. I spent a bit of time, while you were getting him onside, just looking at his DVD collection.

Just as we were finishing, some more visitors arrived, who were introduced as Garth Beckington and his wife. I recognised Garth as a guitarist who had played with Gene at various points along the way, and been part of the band that backed him for his final gigs at the Cinegrill in LA, shortly before his death. Garth needed no persuasion to put his memories of those last days on record.

Jack - I think me and Dan must have been the first ones to speak to him, because we were shooting that big water tower outside Philip's house and Garth came up and started talking to us about the camera. Dan was like "Who's this pissed up nutter?" and I didn't know he was going to be anyone important or someone we were going to interview. We just thought he was some local character, who was going to distract us and try to get involved.

On the way back into town, we stopped off to shoot some more of the idyllic landscapes, before returning to our inn to rendezvous with Jon

Faurot. Jon was another long-time Mendocino immigrant, who'd played with Gene on and off, there and in LA. But his most significant role in the story was as another member of the Cinegrill band and as the man who found Gene's body, in the kitchen of his home in the LA suburb of Sherman Oaks, on 24th May 1991.

The ambient light on the veranda outside our room, from the sun setting over the ocean, was gorgeous. So we put him there, on a rocking chair, with no need for additional lighting.

Dan - Jon Faurot was a strange guy. A bit cloak and dagger. He had secrets he wasn't going to tell us.

Jon seemed fragile – we later found out that he'd also lost his wife quite recently – and the boys reckoned it made it seem we were filming the interview in an upscale care home. Which they felt was appropriate to the elegiac tone of the narrative he'd be recounting. (When I returned to Mendocino with Tricia in 2014, for a screening of the film, Jon joined some other local musicians to play a special set of Gene-related songs at the event. By that time he was, I'm delighted to say, on very good form.)

Day 9 – 19/09 – Mendocino

We'd arranged to interview Kai at his uncle's ranch, a few miles inland. Apparently it was somewhat remote, so he said he'd meet us at the Comptche Store and lead us in. That wasn't hard to find, as the community of Comptche is tiny (a scattered population of less than 200) and the store is the only building of note within it.

While we waited for Kai, enjoying the sunshine and a few minutes of relaxation, an elderly chap came out of the store with his bag of groceries. Clearly unfamiliar faces weren't common in these parts, because he stopped to make a friendly enquiry about what we were doing there. As soon as we mentioned Gene Clark he told us he'd been a roadie for The Flying Burrito Brothers, back in the day, and started regaling us with stories from his wild past. Not just a small town, but a small world!

When Kai arrived – he knew the guy, of course – a few more tales were swapped, before we reluctantly took our leave and followed him through a labyrinth of increasingly small roads and tracks, mostly bounded by thick woods, until we emerged into an area of open pasture and reached the ranch house on a hill overlooking it. It made a fine backdrop for Kai to tell us about his childhood, growing up in these surroundings, which sadly became less idyllic after his parents split up and he found himself dividing time, as his father had, between this rural tranquillity and the hubbub and diversions of LA.

After he'd guided us back to civilisation, we spent the rest of the day roaming the coastline and hills, looking for more shots that would help illustrate the crucial Mendocino chapter of Gene's story.

One of the things that has always excited me most about film making is those unscripted moments, when something both unexpected and perfect happens. We had a few of those moments while shooting this film. One was the glorious sunset that had greeted us with precise synchronisation, as we reached the coast just south of Mendocino for the first time. Another came today, on a stretch of rustic back road where we were doing another quick pick up shot for local atmosphere. We wanted a just a few seconds of empty road, which we were able to get between pauses for the passing of an occasional SUV or truck. Then, just as we were about to move on, over the brow of the hill at the end of the road came an aged jeep, which we tracked until it went by the camera. I don't know what Gene was actually driving, when he came to Mendocino – probably one of the European sports cars that he seemed to favour at the peak of his fame – but this would be an ideal visualisation of that bit of the narrative.

<u>Day 10 – 20/09 – Mendocino > Auburn</u>

Gene's ex-wife Carlie had originally intended to come to Mendocino with Kai and his family. But, as she wasn't in great health, we were now cutting our planned stay on the coast by a day and going to her home in Auburn, about 150 miles east as the crow flies – though a fair bit further than that on the roads that wended their way inland. A return journey through the redwood forests and across the Napa Valley took up the first part of the day.

The diversion wasn't too bad. It was almost on the way to our next appointment on the following day. But Carlie's small house, where we had to shoot the interview, was less than ideal. It had no air conditioning and, on what was the hottest day of the trip so far and without the benefit of the ocean breezes we'd been enjoying, it quickly became stifling. Throw in the heat from a lighting rig, even one as modest as ours, and regular breaks were essential to allow Carlie (and us) to cool down. On top of that, she was the proud owner of a small dog, which kept jumping on and off her lap. A reframing of the shot had to be done, to go in closer on our subject, losing the dog and avoiding continuity issues when editing.

Following the break-up of her marriage with Gene, Carlie had been through some difficult years and had to overcome her own substance abuse issues. After Gene's death she was able to turn her life around and spent the rest of it working with women struggling with the similar challenges. When she passed away, in April 2014, her obituary said "She leaves a legacy of charitable work and helping her fellow man that is impressive and an indication of the type of person she was".

Despite her obvious physical discomfort, Carlie was a wonderfully effervescent, articulate interviewee and was happy to spend the afternoon telling us about her time with Gene – for better and for worse. As someone who'd been one of the Hollywood A Go Go dancers on TV and was working in the music business when she met Gene in 1969, she was also well qualified to comment on the contrasts between their very different lives in LA and Mendocino. Once again, we came away knowing we'd mined a rich seam of material for the film.

Instead of another evening in the charming surroundings of the Little River Inn, we had to make do with the less enticing prospect of Auburn's Comfort Inn. But Dan and Jack were happy to spend a few hours chilling out with the TV and takeout pizza, while I caught up on essential admin and tried to resolve arrangements for the next part of the schedule. Interviews on our return to LA still had to be nailed down and, with Gene's siblings as yet uncommitted to being filmed, plans for our forthcoming excursion to his Missouri homeland were very much up in the air.

Day 11 – 21/09 – Auburn to Kettleman City

We only had one appointment today – an interview with Ken Mansfield in Murphys, a pretty spot in the foothills of the Sierra Nevada, about 100 miles south of Auburn. After that we would be starting the long haul back to LA.

Ken would probably deserve a documentary of his own, having led an extraordinary life in the music business, which took him to places as diverse as the Savile Row rooftop in London, watching The Beatles' final live performance as the manager of Apple Records in the States, and the recording studios of Nashville as a Grammy award winning producer, working with the likes of Waylon Jennings and Willie Nelson. Having suffered some serious lows after that, he then had a life-changing 'born again' experience, which took him on to successful third career as a motivational speaker and author.

We, however, would be asking him about his close friendship with Gene, formed after they had both joined the diaspora of LA music business refugees to Northern California in the early '70s.

Unsurprisingly, he also had an informed viewpoint on the reasons for the downward spiral of Gene's post-Byrds career.

From Murphys it was back to I5 and a long, uneventful drive south through the endless citrus groves that populate California's vast central plain. We stopped for the night in Kettleman City, halfway along the return journey, which consisted of little more than a motel, a gas station and a couple of fast food restaurants, and was a classic example of the American tendency to make a mockery of the word 'city'. Our stay there was distinguished only by Jack's catastrophic demonstration of how not to use a waffle maker, when we had breakfast the next morning.

Day 12 – 22/09 – Kettleman City > LA

Leaving someone else to clear up the mess left by Jack, we continued our journey back to LA – another 300 miles of straight nothingness and searing heat. But at least we covered those miles as quickly as possible and reached our destination in time to grab a quick lunch, before meeting up with David Jackson in the Van Nuys area of town. (Lunches were invariably quick, consisting almost exclusively of drop ins to burger or pizza places and once – never to be repeated! – at Taco Bell. Healthy eating was not the order of the day, but thankfully the amount of energy being expended stopped me from ever feeling like Morgan Spurlock in 'Supersize Me'.)

David had been the bass player in Dillard & Clark, during their relatively brief existence. He was the only member of the band available to be interviewed, as noted earlier, so was essential to telling that part of the story. Fortunately he was another excellent interviewee, with clear recollections of happenings over forty years' time ago and a very engaging way of recounting them. He also had a clear affection and admiration for Gene, which came across very strongly.

We had intended to do one more interview, with Harold Sherrick, the photographer who took the last pictures of Gene before his death. We couldn't find a time that worked for both of us, but he was generous in allowing us to use his shots in the film.

Instead we went to Beachwood Drive, overlooked by the Hollywood sign, in search of the house where Doug Dillard had lived and Dillard & Clark had come together. Apparently it was now a B&B called The Beachwood Canyon Retreat. No-one was in when we knocked on the door, but the lady who runs it got in touch with us later and bought some copies of the DVD to offer her guests. While we were shooting the plant-covered exterior of the 1920s building, a youngish chap came out of the house next door and asked what we were doing. As we explained the history of the place and the reason for our presence, I could sense him losing interest. Gene and Doug may have been LA scene makers back in the day, but they're not exactly on the A list now. The guy disengaged himself as soon as he could do so politely and left us to it.

Day 13 – 23/09 – LA

Our last day in LA was a hectic one, even by the high levels of hecticness that had prevailed, with very few exceptions, thus far.

We started by heading out to Topanga Canyon to interview Al Hersh, who had been tour manager for the later versions of The Byrds and for McGuinn Clark & Hillman in the early to mid-1970s. The Canyon was picturesque but very rustic, so finding his place was a bit tricky.

Al was a battle-hardened veteran of life on the road, who gave us a no-holds-barred account of his experiences during a time when hard drug use was becoming increasingly prevalent in the rock music world. It wasn't only the music and the people making it that suffered – the poor sods trying to run the show undoubtedly had their jobs made much more challenging. Al was pretty brutal in his assessments of the various people involved, which not only provided us with some good quotes but gave what was probably an accurate picture of a period which, while it brought Gene a belated taste of further success, was not the happiest time of his life.

From Topanga we had to dash back to the very different surroundings of Beverley Hills and the offices of Jerry Moss. Jerry had been the M in A&M Records, which had been home to Dillard & Clark and Gene as a solo artist, for a few years in the late '60s and early '70s.

Jack - Jerry Moss's office felt like the classic LA agency building. A big corporate building. Me and Dan had a certain idea about how we wanted it filmed. Him behind his desk with a big plaque saying 'Jerry Moss' or whatever, with some gold discs or something behind him. I wanted each shot to sum up the person in it. So I thought we'd get him behind his big oak desk with platinum discs, which would immediately say 'music mogul'. But he obviously had a very specific idea of what he wanted. We were told by his assistant that it had to be him sitting in front of his big Julian Schnabel painting, which he's obviously very proud of. But it was a really big Schnabel, covering pretty much the whole wall. There was no way we could get it all in, without it being completely out of focus. So in the end we had him and the bottom of his painting.

Although Gene's output had made very little contribution to the label's enormous success (that was due to the likes of Peter Frampton, The Carpenters and The Police), Jerry clearly held Gene's talents in high regard and still had regrets that those talents couldn't be translated into greater record sales. He gave us a warm, thoughtful interview and we knew that his presence in the film would give it added gravitas.

We went back to our hotel to return the lights to the guy who'd hired them to us, recover our deposit (the rig had survived the expedition unharmed) and sort out the rest of our stuff, before heading to the airport to drop off the hire car and start the next leg of our journey.

Day 14 – 24/09 – LA to Missouri

After lengthy debate and negotiation, we'd ended up agreeing to meet with Taj Mahal in Steelville, a small town in rural Missouri, where he was playing a date on his nationwide tour. This was the closest he would get to our planned itinerary, although it was still 250 miles from Kansas City, which is where we wanted to be to visit the places of Gene's upbringing and speak with more members of his family.

Our flight left LAX at 1.05 in the morning. Or rather, our first flight left LAX at 1.05 in the morning. There were no direct flights from LA to Kansas City, so we had to go via Dallas, eventually reaching KC at 9am. There we picked up another hire car and were met by Dan Torchia, our guardian angel in these parts, who had arranged the hire of another lighting rig at a very reasonable price. Barely stopping to exchange courtesies (there would be more time for that when we came back to KC), we loaded up the car and headed through the backwaters of Missouri towards Steelville.

The gig that Taj was doing was in some kind of country club/resort on the outskirts of town. When we arrived he was in his dressing room, doing an interview with the local newspaper, and didn't seem to have any awareness of who we were or why we were there. Once this was explained, he was very amenable and we decided to film him on the stage where he would be performing. Which was a good spot, apart from the fact that the auditorium was right next to the resort's restaurant and bar, where they were just finishing a busy lunchtime service. When Jack and Dan started familiarising themselves with the new gear and setting up, they attracted some curious onlookers. And when Taj came onto the stage to do the interview, the room soon got filled with both people and chatter.

Trying to clear them out seemed likely to cause some ill feeling (no-one tells God-fearing, freedom-loving Americans what to do, especially after a good lunch), so I opted for explaining what we were up to, inviting them to watch and listen while we spoke with Taj, but imploring them to keep quiet. Mention of Gene Clark drew the usual "Who??" reactions, but they turned out to be mostly considerate and co-operative, and noises off were at a level that was just about tolerable.

Dan - We were doing it with him sat on the stage and there were all these people hanging around, which made it a bit weird. There was one bloke who kept guffawing, even when there wasn't anything particularly funny.

Jack - Taj was one of those people who didn't do anecdotes, but had a really good, choice way of phrasing things. It's not like we didn't have any use for him. You almost need someone like that. Not only the way he looked, but his voice and his presence. He gave it a bit of authenticity as well. If you were trying to persuade someone that Gene Clark was a real ground-breaking, trail blazing, cool guy and all you've got is McGuinn and Hillman saying "Oh, he was really cool", then it might be bit "So what?" But if you've also got Taj Mahal on top saying "Yeah, he impressed and influenced me", then you're more likely to go "OK then. Maybe this guy had something."

I would have loved to stay on to enjoy Taj's show, but we were already running on empty after two very full days and a sleepless night, and we had another longish drive heading back west, ready for another early start the next day, so we packed up, said our farewells and moved on. Our motel for the night was in a place called California, for some reason. Apart from the very basic accommodation, it consisted of a gas station and pizza parlour, both of them independently run. Suffice it to say, this California did not remind us of the other one.

Day 15 – 25/09 – Tipton to Kansas City

First stop today was Tipton, about 100 miles east of Kansas City, where Gene was born in his grandparents' house and spent the first couple of years of his life, and where he's buried.

The actual location and continued existence of the house were a matter of debate. John Einarson's excellent biography has it at 304 Morgan, but when we found the street it turned out that there was both a West Morgan and an East Morgan, neither of which seemed to have a number 304. (American addresses in most parts, outside the city centres, are done by their distance in yards from the start of the street or road rather than numbered sequentially. So, for example the house at 300 West Morgan was followed by the next one at 316 West Morgan. This explains why some addresses in more remote areas are numbered in the thousands, even tens of thousands, despite there being no other properties in sight.)

We spoke with a couple of people who were in the vicinity, in the hope of getting some information. The younger of the two knew nothing, while the other one thought there had been an older property there, which had been burned down. Neither of them had heard of their town's most (only?) notable resident.

Gene's family later confirmed that their grandparents' house had indeed stood at 304 East Morgan, but it had been gone for many years, along with the surrounding buildings. "Nothing is the same as it was", they told us.

The cemetery on the outskirts of town was deserted when we got there, but Gene's grave was quite easy to find, thanks to the flowers and other small tributes that adorned it. We spent a few moments in quiet contemplation before shooting some footage of the headstone and its surroundings.

Once we'd reached Kansas City and checked into our hotel, we met up with Dan Torchia again, to discuss plans for the next couple of days. Then made use of the guest laundry, which was very welcome and much needed after two weeks of living out of suitcases without having access to such facilities.

The most important business of the day, however, was a meeting with two of Gene's siblings – older sister Bonnie and younger brother David – in the hope of convincing them to give interviews. Over the years they and the rest of the family had been on the receiving end of a number of approaches about Gene-related projects, all of which started with great enthusiasm and grand ideas, only to evaporate into disappointment. Understandably, they had become both cynical and wary.

As a result, the first few minutes of our time together in the hotel bar were a bit tense. But yet again the fact that I was travelling with two sons and a minimum of palaver, rather than the usual posse of technicians and production assistants, wielding mobile phones and clipboards, seemed to stand us in good stead. I took them through what we'd been doing, which by this time meant we'd already shot a very sizeable percentage of the footage we'd need, and what we wanted to do while we were in Kansas City. It must have done the trick, because they happily agreed to meet up the next day, to shoot the interviews at Bonnie's house in one of Kansas City's outlying suburbs.

Day 16 – 26/09 – Kansas City

Before going to meet Bonnie and David, Dan Torchia took us to the home of Jack Godden, Gene's closest friend during the ten years or so before he left Missouri to join The New Christy Minstrels. As such he was able to give us a good insight into the Clark family's straitened circumstances (Mum, Dad and thirteen kids crammed into a small house buried deep in the woods – a converted trolley barn with no running water or mains power) and into Gene's early development as a musician and songwriter.

Jack told us that he was about to undergo major heart surgery and we had to pause the interview several times, so he could catch his breath and recover his strength to continue. But he was yet another natural storyteller and seemed very much at ease, despite not being accustomed to talking in front of cameras. We were saddened to hear that he'd passed away, not long after we'd met.

Interviewing Bonnie and David presented Dan and Jack with something of a challenge. We wanted to continue our policy of shooting every interview in a different setting, that was specific to the interviewee, but we were filming both of them in Bonnie's house, which was quite small and gave little room for manoeuvre – or setting up of lights. They resolved the problem by putting the camera in the middle of the open plan room that took up most of the ground floor, shooting Bonnie at her kitchen table looking one way and David in an easy chair, seen from the other direction. They both appeared to be in natural home settings, but you'd never have known it was the same home.

Jack - By that point, me and Dan were just able to go in and get set up in about 45 minutes. And in some of those places there weren't many options. In Bonnie's house there was an interesting looking kitchen, so we shot her in that, and there was the living room, where we shot David. That was it. So it wasn't like we could spend a lot of time figuring out options. And it wasn't taking long, after doing two or more a day for the previous three weeks.

The two interviews presented a stark contrast in tone. Bonnie's was wry and bittersweet – unapologetic about the austerity of their upbringing and matter-of-fact about the family's sporadic interactions with Gene after his rise to fame. David, on the other hand, had been much closer to his brother, both in childhood and as adults. The ups and downs of those experiences and the trauma of Gene's passing were clearly still raw. Tears were never far from the surface. As we left Dan Torchia, who had been observing quietly throughout, said how great he thought the interviews had been. We could only agree.

There was still some daylight left, so Dan T took us a little further away from the city, to find some locations that would have been unchanged since Gene's early years. The setting sun gave a beautiful light after a day of clear blue skies – the 'magic hour' that film makers cherish – and we got a variety of footage, both urban and rural that we knew would give us good options in the edit.

Jack - My main reference for landscapes was 'The Assassination of Jesse James by the Coward, Robert Ford' – the sweeping rural scenes. Because that was in Kansas. Obviously if it was now, we'd get someone with a drone. At least for the rural areas – Kansas and Mendocino. But they didn't exist at the time. Or if they did, they would have been very expensive. I doubt there would have just been 'a guy'. Especially in Mendocino.

To reward ourselves after another very successful day and, as a small thank you for his invaluable help, we asked Dan T to suggest a place for a slap-up dinner. He took us to Joe's Kansas City Bar-B-Que, which later appeared on the list of '13 Places to Eat Before You Die', compiled by the late and much-lamented Anthony Bourdain. That's probably about as high a recommendation as you can get and we could only endorse it. We went back to our hotel with filled with great food and with a confidence that what had started out as an optimistic long shot was now well on the way to hitting its target.

Day 17 – 27/09 – Kansas City

We'd got all the interviews we came to Kansas to do, so we had a clear day ('clear' in terms of both schedule and weather) for visiting the various locations around the area, where Gene had spent his formative years. Dan Torchia was our invaluable guide once again.

The house in the woods was long gone, but the rural surroundings of Swope Park were largely unchanged and the nearby railway track, which he'd immortalised in his song 'Kansas City Southern' and in the name of one of his bands, were still there. We moved on to Raytown High School, which Gene attended along with Jack Godden, and then to

Bonner Springs – a more residential suburb, which the Clark family moved to when Gene was 15.

The Bonner Springs house was still there, but no-one was at home when we arrived, so we shot the exterior from the open front lawn. We were looking out from the porch when a hummingbird (which I didn't even know existed in these parts) appeared and came right up to the lens of the camera, hovering for a moment before flying off. We all laughed at the unlikeliness of what had just happened and I jokingly said "It's Gene, just letting us know he's watching",

When I told this story to a friend who believes in such things, she told me that hummingbirds are messengers from loved ones and are often taken as 'totem animals' – creatures that have a special spiritual connection or symbolism in a person's life. A hummingbird totem is seen as representing hope and independence. Which sounded very appropriate for the making of our film.

The other most memorable moment of the day, for entirely different reasons, came when we stopped for a late lunch. A somewhat ramshackle but characterful looking place on a small back road caught our eye, so we pulled over and went in to enjoy some authentic fried chicken. We were too busy eating to have much conversation, but Dan Torchia hardly said a word. When we got back to the car and he'd got in and locked the door, he told us why. Unnoticed by myself or the boys, we were the only white faces anywhere around and apparently the other patrons of the restaurant had been eyeing us up, in a way that he felt was less than friendly. He reckoned it was only our English accents that saved us from attracting more than just glances.

At the end of a very productive day, Dan T took the lighting rig back to its owner and we got ourselves together to move on the next morning.

<u>Day 18 – 28/09 – Kansas City to Orlando</u>

The final stop on our American odyssey was to be Orlando. This hadn't been part of the original plan, but Roger McGuinn – the leader of The Byrds and the band's only ever-present member – lived there and couldn't see us anywhere else, even though he was doing a UK tour only a few weeks later. He (or rather his wife) also declined the suggestion of shooting the interview at their home just outside Orlando, so we would have to find an alternative setting.

Yet again, the journey from Kansas City to Florida wasn't straightforward, taking us via Cincinnati and using up most of the day. It was early evening by the time we reached Orlando and mid evening by the time we'd collected our hire car (with a full tank of petrol which the hire company insisted we pay for, even though we'd only be travelling a few miles in it) and found our hotel.

We'd already arranged the hire of lights for the next day's shoot, thanks to a successful online search for 'Orlando cameraman', but a location that would get the approval of Mr & Mrs McGuinn was still to be identified. I'd hoped that the hotel might have a suitable meeting room, like the one in Frankfurt where we'd shot Barry McGuire and John York. And they did, but at a price that seemed extortionate. Thankfully we had a suite of a size you'd expect in an American resort hotel. So we decided that, with a bit of re-arranging, it could be turned into a film studio. We just told the McGuinns we'd be filming at the hotel and thankfully that was acceptable.

<u>Day 19 – 29/09 – Orlando</u>

Roger wasn't due until 1 o'clock and the guy with the lights was coming in at 12, so we had plenty of time to sort out the room, ready for filming. Actually it was two rooms – a bedroom with two large beds and a living room/kitchenette. We moved as much as we could from the living room into the bedroom, and what couldn't be transferred we shifted so that one end of the room was almost completely clear, apart from a chair and a table with a lamp next to the window. The only downside was that, by the time the cameras and lights had been positioned to best effect, there was nowhere for me to sit behind the camera to do the interview. I ended up crouched in a broom cupboard, in a corner of the room.

Jack - When we got to Orlando, there was the stress of "Where are we going to film?". You had been talking to the hotel about shooting in the conference room or the lobby, because we couldn't go to McGuinn's house. And we wanted the framing, the surroundings of each talking head to reflect their character. Because you don't have a lot of time to establish who each character is, what their personalities are. It's the job of the framing to help do that. Knowing that we were just going to be shooting in an anonymous hotel space, we were trying to figure out how to do that with Roger McGuinn. But we knew that anywhere in the hotel would be basically just a plain wall, so we thought we might as well do it in our room for free, rather than paying hundreds of dollars – which was what the hotel were asking – to do it in a conference room. Fortunately it was a classic Orlando resort hotel and we had a big suite of rooms. Also, luckily, he brought a guitar with him, so he had a prop which instantly established him as a musician. So it worked out in the end.

This weird awkwardness of the setting may have contributed to what would be, by some distance, the most difficult and least satisfactory encounter of the whole project. I became more and more physically uncomfortable and this probably got transferred to Roger, who never comes across as the most laid back individual at the best of times. I'm ashamed to say that I also suspect I was harbouring some ill feeling towards him, partly based on the many reports of his unsympathetic treatment of Gene over the years, and exacerbated by the problems and added costs involved in our getting to this point with him.

Roger came armed with a guitar, which sat on his lap throughout, almost like a shield. A reflection, I couldn't help thinking, of the fact that his skills as a musician are one area where he doesn't have to feel defensive. He was quite happy talking about the formation of The Byrds and their rise to stardom. But he pretty much clammed up when we moved on to look at Gene's departure from the band, and their subsequent encounters in the 1972 Byrds reunion and in the forming of McGuinn Clark & Hillman. This wasn't for lack of trying on my part. As they left, Roger's wife said "That felt more like a police interrogation than an interview".

Dan - During the McGuinn interview the light was bouncing off his guitar, which annoyed me. If I was doing it now, I'd have done it completely differently. I'd have softened the front light and probably bounced another light off the ceiling, rather than having two lights directly on him. A lot simpler and would probably have looked a whole lot better.

Jack - If you played the whole interview, it wasn't the best. But when you chop it up, there were some good bits. Maybe despite himself, he had some good soundbites. And like with David Crosby, it had a different pacing and rhythm to it. Because of what you said beforehand, about them being a bit difficult, I think you were wondering whether we'd get anything useful out of it. But while you were interviewing him I thought "This is going alright". He was happy to open up and he told us some stories.

Once our visitors had departed we restored the rooms to their original condition, packed away the gear and went to lounge by the pool, our work done for now. Little did we know, as we chilled out and ordered more beers, that a major drama would ensue before we got home.

Day 20 – 30/09 – Orlando

On our one free day of the entire trip, I thought Dan and Jack might want to hit one of Orlando's many theme parks or water parks, as a reward for all their efforts. But they seemed to be as out of gas, after three weeks of intensive work and almost non-stop travel, as I was. They opted for a morning by the pool, an afternoon at the nearby crazy golf course, a serious evening meal and an early night.

Day 21 – 01/10 – Orlando to London

After a much-needed good sleep and a lie in, we got ourselves together and headed to the airport for our overnight flight back to London. We checked in at the Virgin Atlantic desk and got our boarding cards, but then had a bit of palaver as the jobsworth at the desk decided one of our carry-on bags was slightly overweight. (When did you last have to weigh your carry-on bag?) This meant a few minutes of opening up all three and moving things around, to meet with official approval, while trying to ignore the tutting of the people behind us.

We still had plenty of time before the flight, so we wandered round the shops for a while before going to the security gates. I produced my passport and boarding pass. So did Dan. But Jack, despite patting himself down and checking his pockets and bag, didn't.

He couldn't remember where he'd put them, but we decided he must have left them at the check-in. We went back there, only to come up empty-handed. Perhaps he'd inadvertently put them down in one of the shops we'd visited. A tour of all of them suggested he hadn't.

By now we were all experiencing a rising sense of panic. A return to the Virgin desk confirmed what we feared. Without these bits of paper, Jack wouldn't be able to board the plane. We would have to buy another ticket but, more crucially, he would have to get a new passport from the British consulate in Orlando which, as this was Saturday evening, wouldn't be open till Monday. The earliest flight thereafter would be on the Monday evening, getting to London on Tuesday morning. As we were due to pick up lighting gear on the Monday, prior to going to Bristol to interview David Crosby on the Tuesday, it would be a considerable understatement to describe this as a bit of a problem.

I sent the boys on a last, desperate retracing of our steps round the airport while I went to lost property, hoping against hope that the documents might have been handed in. They hadn't, so I sank down into a nearby seat and got my phone out of my bag to start making calls about the change of plans.

With all the reorganising of possessions at the check-in desk, my phone had got buried among other stuff, so I had to rummage in search of it. I found the phone near the bottom of the bag, but I also felt something I wasn't expecting. Something that felt very much like a passport. I pulled it out, opened it up and my spirits soared as Jack's face looked back at me. Moments later I also had his boarding pass in my hand and was running back to where I'd agreed to meet up with the boys.

Their arrival coincided with mine and, to any onlookers, the contrast in our expressions must have been stark. Theirs full of gloom and mine totally elated, as disaster was averted.

Jack - I'm surprised it took us so long, with lots of walking around and stressing, before we checked our cabin bags thoroughly. And it was literally just in the nick of time.

The only issue now was getting to the plane before the gate closed, as the departure board was already showing 'Last call'. Some unaccustomed running and shameless queue jumping was required, but we made it with seconds to spare – the gate was deserted, apart from the ground crew ladies sorting out their paperwork ready to move on to their next task. They exchanged a rolling of eyes and shaking of heads, but let us through. Not for the first time (or the last time), I got the feeling someone or something was watching over us.

Elation was replaced by relief, then exhaustion as I took my seat on the plane. I was just grateful that I'd have nothing to do other than eat mediocre food and doze for the next eight hours. Jack was already studying the in-flight entertainment menu as if nothing had happened.

(This episode had a weird resonance, for me. For as long as I can remember, the recurring theme of my dreams has revolved around difficulties and/or crises while travelling. That can mean anything from trying to get to a destination on time, with a horde of unruly small children in tow, to finding myself stranded and alone in remote and forbidding parts. Sometimes the scenarios involve people and places that I recognise, sometimes they have locations and a cast that are completely unfamiliar. As always seems to be the case with dreams, I wake up with the problem unresolved, either with a vivid recollection of what I've just been through or with only fleeting glimpses of the experience. Now here I was, wide awake in the middle of a dreamlike situation – or should that be a nightmare? Thankfully, on this occasion, there was a resolution and it was a happy one.)

Day 22 – 02/10 – Back home

Our flight reached Heathrow right on time and Tricia was waiting at the arrivals gate to ferry us home.

Dan - I don't have any bad memories about that trip. It was intense, but I don't mind hard work. It was just you, me and Jack. The thing I sometimes hate about shoots is people getting over stressed and talking down to each other. And we had a goal, didn't we? Maybe if we were doing a family trip for three weeks and didn't have any particular purpose, maybe that's when the wheels would have fallen off. There was a point to it, there was something we could focus on, there was a through line to it. And we were meeting different people every day, so if you wanted to vent a bit, you could do it about them.

With Leland Sklar at his home in Pasadena.

With Tom Slocum in Santa Barbara.

SHOOTING IN THE UK

The first full day back on home soil was spent sorting out paperwork – invoices, receipts etc – from the past three weeks. Although it was all money going out for now, with not the slightest immediate prospect of getting anything back, I optimistically assumed that some form of accounting would be necessary, somewhere down the line.

One of the many valuable lessons I'd learned, during my years in advertising, was the advisability of getting mundane chores out of the way as quickly as possible, leaving time and headspace for more important matters. At each of the main agencies where I'd worked, there was a requirement to fill out daily activity sheets, so the number crunchers could calculate whether an account was profitable or whether it was burning up too many man/woman hours for too little return. I always did mine at the end of each day, just before leaving the office. Or as soon as I got back, if I'd been away on a shoot. It took about ten seconds to complete an entry for the day.

Most of my colleagues in the creative department, however, dismissed this humble task as unworthy of their refined talents and simply ignored it. Until, that is, the bi-annual memo from the financial director came round, advising them that if the backlog of activity sheets weren't submitted by the end of the week, their expenses claims wouldn't be paid. A mad panic then ensued and all other work stopped for the day, as several months' worth of time spent had to be recalled and documented with at least some degree of credibility. Brains were wracked, diaries were ransacked, workmates were quizzed. I observed these antics with smug amusement.

There was a more immediate cause for satisfaction, once I'd done all the organising and totting up of the financial side of our jaunt, as I realised that even my parsimonious expectations had been exceeded.

USA shoot costs		Projected	Actual
London > LA plus return from Orlando	£650 per person	£1950	1975.36
LA > Kansas	£125 per person	£375	275.10
Kansas > Orlando	£125 per person	£375	259.20
Accommodation	£150 per night x 20	£3000	1708.23
Subsistence	£100 per day x 21	£2100	1034.94
Car Hire	2.5 weeks @ £250pw	£625	629.49
Petrol		£250	420.67
Equipment hire		£800	550.63
Travel insurance		£100	80.04
Sundries		£150	28.34
Total cost		£9725	£6657.90

The other job for the day was driving down to the hire company in Kingston Upon Thames, to pick up the lighting rig for our interview with David Crosby. I left this as late as possible, before their closing time, to give us a sporting chance of getting it back to them at the same time next day, to avoid going into another 24 hour hire period. We'd done well with the budget so far, but I wasn't inclined to start getting casual. We still had a long way to go.

David Crosby

The Colston Hall was a fine concert venue in Bristol, built in the Victorian era. It still is a splendid edifice, though it's now called The Bristol Beacon. Edward Colston, formerly known as a merchant, philanthropist and politician with many landmarks around the city commemorating him, has become *persona non grata* due to his extensive involvement in the 17ᵗʰ and 18ᵗʰ century slave trade. Most if not all mentions of his name have been erased and his statue, which once overlooked the heart of the city, ended up being torn down and tossed into the harbour by protesters.

I'd spent a great evening at the hall some forty years earlier, watching The Mahavishnu Orchestra perform extraordinary feats of musical stamina and dexterity. Now I was going back to shoot one of our most important interviews. David Crosby was on tour with Graham Nash, his longstanding partner in song, and this had been deemed the most appropriate time and place for a meeting. There were other stops on their itinerary that would have been more convenient for us, but after the trouble we'd had making contact with David's people and the various changes of plans along the way, we weren't about to make waves.

Thankfully the venue's management was quite happy for us to film there, without asking for any remuneration, and suggested we could use one of the smaller theatres in the complex, which wouldn't be needed that afternoon. It proved to be an excellent suggestion and we set up to position our subject with the stage, complete with grand piano and curtains, behind him.

Jack - I didn't really know his music but I knew that David Crosby was a big name and he had been on The Simpsons, so to me that meant he was a big star. But when he walked into the auditorium where we interviewed him, he didn't have any people around him. He didn't have an entourage or anything. He just walked in on his own and sat there. I was surprised about that, because he was the biggest celebrity we were interviewing. It was obviously a good surprise, but it was a surprise. Whenever you meet a celebrity, they always seem smaller in real life. He was just a little old man sitting on a chair, in the end. I noticed he seemed less sympathetic than others to Gene's drug and alcohol problems. But that's probably because he'd had plenty of his own. He was probably thinking "Thank God it wasn't me!". He spoke about it in a very matter of fact way.

David was a very seasoned interviewee – apart from six decades of interactions with the media, he seems to crop up in half the music documentaries that have ever been made – and was at the stage of life where his legacy had become increasingly important to him. Like Roger McGuinn, he was very forthcoming and entertaining when talking about the formation and meteoric success of The Byrds. He was generous in his assessment of Gene's importance to the band. And he was brutally self-critical about the shortcomings of the reunion album, for which he'd assumed the role of producer. But, again like Roger, he became more guarded when the conversation turned to Gene's departure from the band. In fact his answers became so measured that Jack would have something of a challenge, editing out lengthy pauses while keeping the flow of the film, and his contribution to it, running smoothly.

Jack - There were times when, with him and McGuinn – like when Gene walked off the plane – where I would have thought they'd be a bit more evasive about that, because it makes them look... in the way they told it, they don't come across in the most flattering light. Especially because they both remembered that particular quote – "You can't be a Byrd if you can't fly". They both, in different ways, repeated it as if it was a funny line. Do you not realise you're coming across like arseholes here? I was surprised that there were some things they did clam up about, but they didn't clam up about that.

Our most celebrated participant gave us some great material, though. And we made it back to Kingston in the nick of time, before the lighting hire company shut their doors for the night and we were into an extra day of charges. So, all in all, another good day's work.

Jack - I remember getting home from the States and thinking "That was intense, but I can chill now". But then we had to go and see Crosby the next day. He gave us longer than I thought he was going to do. Again, we were wondering what we were going to get out of him and went in with low expectations. But as it went on I thought "Well, he seems to be opening up. There's useful stuff here." He did abruptly end it, all of a sudden. He must have had an idea in his own head of how long he wanted to give us. Because he literally said "I think we're done now" and got up to go. But he let Dan take a portrait shot, before he left.

David Crosby at The Colston Hall (photo by Dan Kendall).

The final interviews: Sid Griffin and Johnny Rogan

We still had two interviews that we knew we had to do. Both very important ones, with guys who had detailed knowledge of the Gene Clark story and would be able to cover all aspects of it. We were banking on them to fill any gaps in the narrative left by the other interviewees.

We wanted to do them both on the same day, in London, to keep equipment hire and travel costs to a minimum. So we had to wait for Johnny to emerge from his remote Irish lair, which ended up not being until November. Fortunately Sid was available around the same time, so we did them on the 7th, hiring the same lighting rig that we'd taken to Germany and Bristol.

We interviewed them at their homes in London, only discovering later how privileged we were, to be granted access to Johnny's flat, a stone's throw from Victoria Station. Apparently people who had known him for years, and considered themselves to be close friends, had never seen inside the place. The interviews were everything we had hoped for – extensive, insightful and engaging. We left, knowing we'd now got all the essential building blocks we'd need.

Jack - When we got to Sid and Johnny, because they were both giving more of an overview/analysis of his career and I had more idea of the story by now, it was more interesting to listen to the interviews. At first, particularly when we were in America, I pretty much spent the entire time while you were interviewing the people looking at the framing or making sure the sound was alright, thinking about other things. I was almost blocking out what they were saying. Whereas by the time we got to Sid and Johnny, I was actually listening to what they were saying. So even though they were talking for a couple of hours, it was all interesting stuff.

With those interviews done, our filming was complete and we could start the lengthy process of editing and firming up on the sourcing and licensing of archive material and music.

Having said that, I have to admit to a small degree of cheating in the authenticity of some of the footage (sorry if this comes as a disappointment). As we put together the chapter about Gene's early years in the rural outskirts of Kansas City, we realised that a bit more footage of locations related to his childhood surroundings would come in handy. Going back to the States to get it was, of course, out of the question. But, fortunately enough, we live on the edge of the Chiltern Hills (to the north west of London, if you're unfamiliar with English geography), which have woodlands not dissimilar to those where the young Clarks whiled away their leisure hours. So we spent a sun-kissed afternoon filming fallen trees, leafy meadows and babbling brooks and, most particularly, the lone skeleton of a tree that had been struck by lightning.

Snippets of that day's work appear at several points in the film – look out for them next time you watch it. And please remember that using one location to represent another has been commonplace in film making at all levels. Almeria in Spain for remote parts of America in Sergio Leone's spaghetti westerns, for example, or the fortifications of Malta for Ancient Rome in 'Gladiator'. We've simply continued that practice.

PUTTING IT ALL TOGETHER

I don't know that much about how other documentary makers start constructing their projects, but we viewed it as a process with four separate elements: 1) Developing a basic narrative script from the interviews we'd filmed and older ones that we'd found; 2) Sourcing archive material – photos, film clips and other appropriate visuals; 3) Identifying the 'B roll' footage of landscapes and other locations, that we'd want to use; and 4) Deciding on the music that should be in the film. Those elements would be blended to make the film.

At this stage, having just completed all the principal filming, we were still hoping that someone with more experience and connections and resources would come on board at some point, to help us through the many challenges of getting the film out into the world. As things turned out, that never happened and actually making the film was the easiest (and quickest) part of the whole exercise.

We (or rather I) found ourselves sourcing and negotiating usage of all the archive material and recordings; learning about DVD production, once we'd chosen that as the first channel for releasing the film; creating the DVD and its packaging; promoting and selling it; arranging for the film to be shown by the BBC; and, of course, paying all the bills. Record labels, publishing companies, photographers, film archives, distributors, production companies, the royalty collection agencies, broadcasters, designers, DVD manufacturers, printers... everything and everybody ended up on my list of things to do.

But all that was for later. To be honest, had I known at the start that I would have to do everything myself, I would almost certainly have been too intimidated to take it on. When I see the credits rolling at the end of other documentaries, even quite modest ones, listing the scores of people involved in different tasks, I marvel at what we achieved with such minimal previous experience and outside assistance.

With the interviews in the can, barring any unexpected late additions, Jack gave me audio files of everything, so I could start the lengthy process of transcribing them, along with the archive recordings that we'd been given. That basic task would have been accomplished much more quickly, if we'd simply handed them over to a copy typist. But, apart from wanting to save money wherever possible, I knew from previous experience that doing the job myself, however ponderously, was a great way of really immersing myself in the raw material and starting to shape it.

There were well over 40 hours of interviews to work through, so it was indeed a lengthy process. Once done, however, I was able to put together a first paper edit quite quickly, so Jack could start work on the actual assembly. This first draft was well over two hours long, even before any other content was put in, and plodded horribly. Fortunately I'd spent enough time in edit suites, watching other films of various lengths being made, to know that this was only to be expected and that the moulding of the raw material into its finished shape was both the most essential and one of the most satisfying parts of the film making process. So we didn't panic or lose faith. We just got on with that moulding.

Exploring the archives

We'd known from the start that Gene Clark lived and worked in a time before everyone carried the ability to shoot hi res stills and video in their coat pocket. Throw in the fact that he was the most camera shy of stars and it was inevitable that there wouldn't be a mountain of archive material at our disposal. Especially once he'd left The Byrds and ceased to be newsworthy.

Which was OK. We couldn't have afforded the rights to a mountain of archive material, even if it existed. Our main concern was finding enough to cover the span of his life and career, to give a feel for the man and his context – both social and environmental – and to make the film as engaging and watchable as possible.

As soon as we knew this was a project we wanted to pursue, I'd started looking for photos, film footage and any other memorabilia that might be available. It was a search that would go on for two years, right up to the point where we committed to a final edit, as we tried to find stuff that would fill gaps in the visual narrative or enhance it.

The film side of things was pretty straightforward. We'd already sourced the clips of The New Christy Minstrels and, of course, we had the priceless Tom Slocum home movie footage, which would give the film its conclusion. There was also quite a bit of Byrds TV performances in various film libraries. But after Gene flew the coop in January 1966, there was then a ten year gap without anything on film until McGuinn Clark & Hillman came along in the mid '70s. That band had done a handful of TV shows in America and Holland, which had survived the culling of archives that TV stations seem all too prone to do. And Gene had made a couple of appearances on 'Nashville Now' with Carla Olson, towards the end of his life.

The question was deciding which bits of this relatively limited range of options we wanted to use and hoping we could afford them.

Lucky break #7

One of the libraries that had Byrds footage was Research Video, a Los Angeles company owned by Paul Surratt. Paul was also a musician who had briefly been in a folk group called The Shilos, alongside Gram Parsons. He had many connections on both sides of the Atlantic, including some of my old Zigzag colleagues. He was very sympathetic to the project and allowed us to use the material we homed in on, from several TV shows, at what can certainly be described as 'mate's rates'. Sadly he had a heart attack in 2012, which left him severely incapacitated, and he passed away in 2020.

But we were able to get a copy of the DVD to him, which we were told he enjoyed.

Lucky break #8

Not long after we got back from the States, I was idly browsing YouTube to see if there was any new Gene-related stuff on there, and came across something headed 'Byrds Gene Clark Home Of A Great Interview'. This turned out to be some home movie footage – quite a bit of it – put up by a guy called Larry Wagner. Back in 1988 he'd been responsible for taking Gene, along with Randy Meisner from (The) Eagles and Rick Roberts, of The Burritos and Firefall, on a tour of radio stations in the Seattle area. They were promoting a concert that some friends of Larry's were putting on. He'd taken his video camera with him and accumulated around 50 minutes of footage, showing the guys doing interviews, chatting with fans and hanging out in their limo. I reached out to him, through his YouTube channel, and got a prompt, friendly response. Apparently he'd been talking with Paul Surratt about licensing the material through Research Video and already knew about our project, which he was very happy to help with. His footage was invaluable in accompanying the '80s chapter of Gene's story, which was otherwise somewhat short of archive content.

Photos also weren't in plentiful supply. The Byrds were obviously much photographed at the peak of their fame, but thereafter shots became increasingly limited. The big photo libraries had a reasonable selection of relevant images, though the prices they charged would mean we could only afford ones that we considered essential. Apart from that, however, what we really wanted were some more intimate, 'unofficial' shots, and stuff that hadn't been seen before. Thankfully, through various channels, we made a few good connections:

Henry Diltz was almost the house photographer of the LA music scene from the late '60s onwards. His album covers for Crosby Stills & Nash and The Doors, in particular, are iconic. He'd done a few shoots with Gene, shortly after he left The Byrds and again around the time of the reunion album. He's a lovely guy, as you can tell from his many music documentary appearances, and he was generous in allowing us to use several of his shots at very preferential rates.

Nurit Wilde was another who was a part of various musicians' friendship groups and turned that access into a career in photography. She'd captured Dillard & Clark's notorious debut at The Whisky and, like Henry, was sympathetic to the project in the usage fees she charged.

Gary Nichamin was the man who photographed Gene most in the later years of his life, from the moment he met Carla Olson on the stage of Madame Wong's in LA, right through their collaborations together. Gary had passed away in 2003, but Saul Davis was looking after his photographic estate and very kindly gave us access to the images that would be fundamental in illustrating that chapter of the film.

Lucky break #9

Nicholas Wilson is a photographer based in Mendocino. Very early on in my search for archive material (May 2011, to be precise), I googled 'Mendocino photos 1970s' and up popped his book, 'Mendocino In The Seventies'. Along with a website that clearly showed he was not only still with us, but still active. Thinking he might be able to provide us with shots that would give a feel for the place, at the time that Gene was living there, I pinged him an email. And got a very prompt reply that exceeded my wildest expectations:

"Gene and Carly Clark lived across the street from me for a while in the early seventies, and I did a publicity photo session for him at his home. It was an ocean bluff house on North Lansing St., Mendocino. I may also have a few scattered performance shots of him in local venues. I haven't seen any of those shots in decades. They exist only as B&W negatives in my files. It would take some time to find the negs, and then they would have to be scanned. I would need a research fee of $100 and a guarantee of a minimum of $100 in usage fees at per second rates to pursue it."

This was, of course, too good an offer to resist. We paid the $100 research fee and met up with Nicholas while we were in Mendocino, to see what he'd managed to unearth – the shots of Gene that he'd mentioned, as well as ones of local landmarks. Once we got home there was a lengthy series of exchanges, sorting out the technical and financial sides of things, and we ended up using five of his images, which were an invaluable accompaniment to the Mendocino chapter of the film.

As an added bonus, we were able to introduce him to a record company who were putting out an album of the demos for Gene's 'White Light' album from 1971. ('Here Tonight' on Omnivore Recordings, if you're interested.) Omnivore were delighted to find previously unseen photos from that era of his life and used one of them as the cover shot, in return for which Nicholas gave us a discount on the usage fee we'd agreed with him. Every little helps.

We also scoured the internet and found a variety of shots, of Gene at different stages of his career and of people and places related to it, and were able to track down at least some of the people who had either taken them or now owned them.

Two treasure troves

In addition to all of the above, we came across two great sources of previously unseen material. One of which we'd been forewarned about and expected to explore, while the other was a wonderful surprise, coming quite late in the day and completely out of the blue.

When we spoke with Barry Ballard, the afore-mentioned Byrds archivist, he mentioned another chap who was, it seemed, even more dedicated in his pursuit of anything Byrds-related. He was an American called Whin Oppice and he had, by all accounts, amassed a quite remarkable stash of memorabilia and archive material – everything from demo tapes and limited editions to photos and assorted ephemera.

I emailed Whin as soon as we got back from the shoot in the States, and so began an exchange of messages that went on for many months, as we identified what Whin had in his stash, what we would be interested in and how it could get to us in a form we could use.

Two things became apparent early on: 1) Like many folk of advancing years (myself included), Whin was not the most tech savvy of chaps, so getting copies of photos and film clips across the Atlantic in digital form would be a challenge. Unsurprisingly, he wasn't willing to let the originals out of his safe keeping, so copies had to be made and transferred. And 2) having spent not inconsiderable sums of money on his collection, he wasn't going to just give us stuff, regardless of how excited he was about our film. Both these issues contributed significantly to the volume of emails between us.

We weren't interested in any of the audio material that Whin had. Even if some of it was great (and by all accounts there are lots of fabulous Gene Clark recordings out there, waiting to be heard, from cassettes made in his kitchen to unreleased studio tapes). We knew that trying to include any such stuff would open up a Pandora's box of ownership issues and potential lawsuits. Especially as Scott Johnson had warned us that they would be particularly sensitive about which of Gene's recordings we would be using.

In the end we narrowed things down to a collection of photos, taken by a long-deceased photographer called John Dietrich, at the No Other recording sessions and in Mendocino; and some silent film footage of The Byrds backstage at the Hullabaloo club on Sunset Strip, which we were told had been shot by their manager, Jim Dickson. This showed Gene apparently running through a song with other members of the band and was a perfect fit with the section of the film where Chris Hillman and David Crosby spoke about his prolific songwriting and its importance to the early success of the band.

Lucky Break #10

The second treasure trove came in the form of a package from Garth Beckington, who we had briefly met and interviewed in Mendocino. That meeting had been unexpected and so was the package, which arrived in October 2012, when we were very close to completing the editing of the film. I could only assume that when I emailed Philip Oleno, to ask if he had any photos of Gene's Mendocino years, he'd passed the request on to Garth and got my address from Kai Clark.

As soon as I saw what was in the package, I knew the editing period would have to be extended. There were a number of photos, polaroids and prints, showing the outside of Gene and Carlie's house in Albion and assorted gatherings inside it. Although most of them were a bit damaged and none of them were great photos, that almost seemed to make them more appropriate, as a record of a time when the Mendocino idyll was turning sour and Gene's life was falling apart. We were struggling for visual material to illustrate that part of the film, so this was an absolute godsend.

The other item was a DVD, containing film of Gene doing a solo, acoustic rendition of 'Silver Raven' from the 'No Other' album. It wasn't clear when this was shot, but judging by his somewhat haggard appearance I would hazard a guess at the mid to late '80s. Gene wasn't in great shape, but it was a compelling performance, which we knew would make a perfect segue into the full recorded version.

The songs

One of the non-negotiable first principles of our project was the inclusion of a good range of Gene's music, from all stages of his career. And we knew that getting permission to use that music, and paying for it, would be the most demanding of the many tasks we would have to undertake.

Unfortunately my friend (still my friend) Chris, who had been persuaded to take on this particular responsibility, had come to his senses and realised that any remuneration he might get, even if by some miracle there were profits to be shared with him, would in no way reflect the time and effort he'd have to put in. So he gracefully withdrew. But not before passing on some of his hard-earned wisdom about the minefield that is the music royalties system.

These royalties can be earned in a number of ways. When records and CDs are sold. When a recording is broadcast. When it's played in public – at a disco, for example, or in a live performance. When it's used in an advert. When it's used in a video game – an increasingly common and profitable source of income. When it's played on a streaming service, such as Spotify – an increasingly common and unprofitable source of income. When it's published as sheet music – an increasingly uncommon source of income. And, of course, when a recording is used in a TV show or a film.

Essentially, they fall into two categories. Publishing royalties, which are earned by the writer(s) of a song or piece of music and are administered by the publishing company that owns the rights to the material. And master royalties, which relate to an actual recorded performance of that material. These are earned by the artist(s) who made the recording and are administered by their record company. So, for example, publishing royalties for 'All The Young Dudes' would go to David Bowie and his publishers, while the master royalties for Mott The Hoople's recording of the song would go to the band and their record label.

We would have to identify and deal with companies on both sides of the equation. Of which there would be many, as we were hoping to use extracts from several dozen songs in the film, and Gene had left a tangled web of record labels and publishing companies, large and small, in his wake.

Here are the songs we had on our wish list, in the order they appear over the course of the film. Chosen either because they tied in with a particular part of the narrative or because – at least in my opinion – they showed Gene's music at its considerable best.

Eight Miles High – Perhaps Gene's most instantly recognisable song, although to get it recorded he had to share writing credits with McGuinn, for the arrangement, and Crosby, who apparently contributed one line of the lyrics. With its influences from jazz and Indian music, it's seen as a genuinely ground-breaking landmark and should have been a much bigger hit, if it hadn't been banned by many radio stations, who took the title as referring to drugs rather than a plane flight to London.

Kansas City Southern – One of several of Gene's songs which were directly inspired by his childhood experiences. It refers to the rail network that ran (and still runs) close to the Clark family home in Swope Park. We went to the tracks that Gene would almost certainly have played alongside and shot some footage that appears in the film. Gene also took the name for the band that he formed with Tommy Kaye, to promote the 'Two Sides To Every Story' album, and which he brought to the UK in 1977, when I met him.

Something's Wrong – Another song reflecting his rural upbringing, though this one is more about his environmental concerns as an adult. One of several great songs on the first Dillard & Clark album.

Blue Ribbons – One of the first songs Gene wrote, as a teenager. Kai had managed to get hold of the reel-to-reel tape, which was found in the

Clark family home in Kansas City after his father's death. As it had never had a public airing, the estate wanted to protect their interest in the whole song, but we got permission to use a segment of it. Which was fine for the film, although it would have been nice to have been able to include the full version as an added extra on the DVD. The recording was allegedly made when Gene was just fourteen, although his voice sounds remarkably mature for one so young. It's possible that it was re-recorded when he was somewhat older.

Green Green – The New Christy Minstrels' biggest hit, recorded before Gene joined the group. This was the song that gave us a perfect editing segue from Barry McGuire's performance in Germany to the archive clip of the group on the Hootenanny TV show.

Run The Ridges – The song that Gene was performing with The Surf Riders, when he was discovered by The New Christy Minstrels in a Kansas City bar. This is the original version by The Kingston Trio, one of many groups riding the early 60s folk wave, and the starting point in the career of John Stewart, another great American singer/songwriter.

Julianne – A traditional folk song of the type that was one half of the Minstrels' stock-in-trade. The half that Gene found more acceptable.

Billy's Mule – And the other half. A prime example of what Barry McGuire referred to as the "silly little ditties', written by group founder Randy Sparks, which were definitely not what Gene wanted to sing.

Drinking Gourd (Muddy Road To Freedom) – Another traditional song, which Gene was able to perform with conviction, as captured on another Hootenanny clip which appears in the film.

Feel A Whole Lot Better (Byrds) – Perhaps Gene's finest Byrds era song, appearing on *Rolling Stone*'s '500 Greatest Songs Of All Time' list. It was the B-side of the band's second single and has been covered by a range of artists over the years. Most notably by Tom Petty (see below).

Mr Tambourine Man (Byrds) – The Bob Dylan song that The Byrds transformed, launching them to stardom and becoming the template for the whole folk rock movement. A worldwide Number One for the band, this would be a central part of The Byrds chapter of the film.

She Don't Care About Time – Another major part of The Byrds' catalogue, this was the B-side to their second chart topper, 'Turn Turn Turn', so made a significant contribution to Gene's earnings from royalties – something that quickly had a damaging impact on relationships within the group.

Echoes – The most ambitious track on Gene's multi-faceted debut solo album from 1967, arranged by Leon Russell. A level of production that Gene wouldn't attempt again until 'No Other' in 1974.

Tried So Hard – One of the songs on that first solo album that really supports Gene's claim to be among the foremost pioneers of country rock. Rumoured to have been inspired by his fleeting affair with Michelle Phillips, from The Mamas & The Papas.

With Care From Someone – A highlight from the first Dillard & Clark album. A perfect marriage of Gene's songwriting and Doug's world class picking.

Train Leaves Here This Morning – Written with Bernie Leadon, during their time together in Dillard & Clark, Bernie took it with him and sang it on the first Eagles album, which sold over a million copies. A nice boost for Gene's earnings from royalties in the '70s, when income from other sources was starting to dry up.

1975 – One of the less celebrated songs from the 'White Light' album. But it made an ideal soundtrack for the sequence of location footage that Jack put together, to transition Gene's move from the hurly-burly of LA to the tranquillity of Mendocino.

For A Spanish Guitar – An extraordinary piece of work, that Bob Dylan said he would have been proud to have written. Probably my favourite Gene song, in the face of very stiff competition.

The Virgin – Another track from the beautifully restrained 'White Light'. Almost certainly about his new relationship with Carlie, his soon-to-be wife. That's what we used it to illustrate, anyway.

White Light – What was originally meant to be the title track of Gene's first solo album for A&M, until the art department omitted to put those words on the cover. But it's generally known by that title anyway. Philip Oleno, Gene's friend in Mendocino, reckons the song is about his place in the woods of Northern California, where he had a blacksmith's forge.

I Remember The Railroad – Back to the scenes of Gene's rural childhood and another wistful recollection of happier times. This was one of the songs recorded for the follow-up to 'White Light'. They were shelved by A&M, when they ran out of patience with Gene's reluctance to do promotional work. They only got disinterred from the vaults when the Dutch arm of the company decided to release them as the 'Roadmaster' album, in recognition of Gene's strong following in the Netherlands, padded out to LP length with a couple of earlier out-takes.

Full Circle – The first of two songs that Gene contributed to The Byrds' 1973 reunion album on Asylum. By general consensus the best things on it, along with the Neil Young and Joni Mitchell songs, as the others kept their better stuff for their solo work and brought in rubbish such as 'Born To Rock'n'Roll'.

Changing Heart – And the second one. Gene also sang lead on two of the three cover versions, which they resorted to, in order to fill out the album. All of which convinced David Geffen to sign him to Asylum, resulting in the magnificent, but ill-fated 'No Other' album.

Silver Raven – Talking of which, here's one of the standout tracks from that album. We merged two versions in the film – a clip of Gene performing it solo with just an acoustic guitar for accompaniment, which was among the package of goodies that Garth Beckington gave us, transitioning into the sumptuous production that's on the album.

No Other – Fine as it is, this probably wouldn't have been my first choice for another track from the 'No Other' album…'Some Misunderstanding' is one of my top three Gene Clark songs. But Lee Sklar told a good story about his bass playing contribution to it, so it had to go in.

Silent Crusade – The first of three songs from the 'Two Sides To Every Story' album. A real curate's egg, imho, featuring some of Gene's best songs – most notably the ones that we used – and some cover versions that sit awkwardly alongside them.

Hear The Wind – Written in the aftermath of Gene's break up with Carlie, it's hardly surprising that the original songs on 'Two Sides' are suffused with wistfulness and regret.

Past Addresses – See above.

Backstage Pass – Of the four songs that Gene contributed to the first McGuinn, Clark & Hillman album, this was by some distance the best,

Don't You Write Her Off – Written by Roger McGuinn, not by Gene. This was MC&H's solitary hit, so it was what they were performing in the TV clips that we found. If you look for those clips on YouTube, you'll see some clear, and unintentionally hilarious, illustrations of the tensions that plagued the band and contributed to their early demise.

Mr Tambourine Man (Gene Clark) – Gene did his own version of The Byrds' signature song for the 'Firebyrd' album, which was recorded in 1982 but not released until 1984. It was later remixed and reissued as 'This Byrd Has Flown'.

Rain Song – Also from the 'Firebyrd' album, this was the one song that was meant to be in the film but had to be pulled at the last minute, as we weren't able to get clearance for it. It was co-written with Andy Kandanes, who produced the album, but he had passed away in 2010. Despite making contact with the record labels that had released different versions of the album, with his family and even with his solicitor, we were never able to confirm who owned his share of the publishing. Using the song without that information and their approval would have been too risky, especially as it wasn't central to the film.

Del Gato – Co-written with his brother Rick, this was one of the standout tracks on the studio album that Gene made with Carla Olson, 'So Rebellious A Lover'. Carla said she thought it was an old standard when she first heard it, and it does have a timeless feel to it. When the film came out and we had made contact with a recovering Rick, bless him, he wondered if its inclusion might lead to a royalties windfall. This seemed highly unlikely, but it should at least earned him a few extra dollars – so long as his publishing company is doing its job properly.

Gypsy Rider – Another one of my favourite Gene songs. This was also from the album with Carla and we were able to source a clip of them doing a good job of performing it on the 'Nashville Now' TV show with the house band, even though Gene didn't look in great shape.

Carry On – Originally written for the 'Karate Kid Part II' movie, this was one of many songs recorded by CRY (Clark Robinson York) in the late '80s. It was included on the 'Under The Silvery Moon' album, which first came out in 2001 and was soon embroiled in legal issues, as approval for the release hadn't been given by Gene's estate. The lyrical theme, of struggling on in the face of adversity and disappointment, pretty much sums up his final years.

Feel A Whole Lot Better (Tom Petty) – The recording that financed Gene's final demise, through his return to bad habits. When Tom backed out of being interviewed, we were concerned that we wouldn't be allowed to have it in the film. Thankfully, after sending his management a clip showing the context in which we were using it, we got the OK.

I Shall Be Released - The other Dylan song on the list, which Gene and his friends were singing in the previously unseen home movie footage that we'd been given. This clip had been earmarked, from the very start, as the conclusion and emotional climax of the film.

Jack – It's interesting that you only wanted to use the songs that were chronologically appropriate. We only used the songs that were released at the time we were talking about or which related to that particular time. But they all fitted perfectly to the mood and the tone of the period, and to the narrative. Which shows how Gene wrote songs that encapsulated him at any given time.

As I started contacting the various publishing companies and record labels, who owned the rights to these songs, I soon came across a term that I'd never heard before but which would assume great significance – 'most favoured nations'.

Essentially this means that whatever terms have been contractually agreed must be changed, if appropriate, so that they match the most favourable deal struck by somebody else for the same service. An appearance fee, for example. Or, in this case, use of a song. All the music copyright holders, as well as some of the more savvy interviewees, had a 'most favoured nations' clause in their contracts with us.

Which wasn't a problem, at first. None of our interviewees were being paid, so appearance fees weren't an issue. And my philosophy of "ain't too proud to beg", combined with the quite justifiable contention that we would be shining a light on an artist who had been all but forgotten about by the various people and companies who had an interest in his work, was delivering a good outcome, when it came to agreeing a price for use of the songs with publishers and record labels.

I'd manage to get fees for all the songs that Gene had written, on his own or with co-writers, down to a level that was just about affordable. But then we hit a roadblock that threatened to fundamentally damage, or even derail, the whole project.

Negotiations with Bob Dylan's publishers in the UK, for permission to use 'Mr Tambourine Man' and 'I Shall Be Released', did not go well. They took the position, not unreasonably, that these were two of the greatest songs by one of the greatest songwriters. Even for our quite modest usage, they were quoting sums that ran into many thousands. Just getting those two songs, at those prices, would have been out of our reach. But of course, even if we'd been able to afford that, it would have triggered everyone else's 'most favoured nations' clause and pushed the total cost of music licensing into the hundreds of thousands. All arguments and pleading made not an iota of difference. They'd never heard of us, they'd never heard of Gene Clark, they were looking after the interests of a very celebrated client and they weren't going to budge.

Lucky Break #11

If you remember back to the early days of the project, we'd been given the email address of Dylan's manager, Jeff Rosen, which we'd optimistically used to explore the possibility of getting an interview. We hadn't been disappointed when that came to nothing, as we didn't have any real expectation of success, but we were now facing what would be a massive blow to our ambitions for the film. So I sent Mr Rosen another email message one evening, explaining the situation and politely asking if there was anything he could do to resolve the impasse.

When I woke up the next morning, a reply was waiting for me. It copied in their guy at the US end of their publishing company, instructing him to agree the same terms for the two Dylan songs as we'd achieved for all the others. With one bound we were free. There were many moments of joy, while we were making the film, but this was without doubt the most exhilarating. My sense of relief and of stunned delight, as I read that email, can't be overstated.

GETTING IT OUT THERE

As we neared completion of the editing process, during the back end of 2012, we started paying serious attention to how the film might be released and putting out feelers to people who we hoped would help with that. Distributors, in particular, on both sides of the Atlantic.

Our first thought had been to start by taking it to film festivals, in the hope that this would give us exposure and attract interest from media and other relevant companies, as well as audiences; then arranging TV broadcasts; and eventually a DVD release – maybe even BluRay, if there seemed to be enough demand – which would ideally be timed to tie in with any broadcast screenings. Streaming, through sites such as Netflix or Amazon Prime, wouldn't become a consideration until some while later. In 2012 Netflix was still about DVD rentals, first and foremost, and had only just launched its streaming service in the UK, with a limited range of content. Amazon Prime was still focused largely on delivery of orders. And the plethora of streaming services, that we now have, were still several years away.

A number of factors forced a reassessment of this plan, however. We soon discovered that public screenings of the film would require theatrical licences from the various record labels and publishers, who owned the rights to all the music. And those owners wanted to treat any public showing, whether it was a one-off at a small festival or a simultaneous release in every cinema in the known world, in the same way. And price the licences accordingly. Since our intentions revolved around just a limited number of film festivals, which would generate little or no income, this was clearly a non-starter.

The same issue looked like putting the kibosh on broadcast screenings. Broadcast licences, whether bought on a global basis or territory by territory, were also well beyond our limited means and were highly unlikely to be covered by whatever a TV company (certainly the smaller ones) might pay us for the privilege of showing it.

Producing the DVD

Once we'd decided on a DVD run as the best way of getting the film out there (and hopefully refilling at least some of the big hole in our bank account), we had to embark on yet another steep learning curve. We owned many DVDs between us but, like most people, took them for granted as one more miracle of technology and had little idea what went into actually producing them.

A quick internet trawl soon identified several companies in the London area who might be worth approaching for advice and assistance, and recommendations from friends and associates – not least Start Productions, who had gone down exactly the same path before us – narrowed that list down to a manageable number. After speaking with them and milking their wisdom, we realised that a number of decisions would need to be made as a first step.

How many copies should we order? Unsurprisingly, the bigger the print run the lower the unit cost. But we needed to find some sort of balance between that economy and a realistic expectation of sales. An expectation which we had no real way of gauging with any confidence.

How should the DVD be packaged? From looking at our own collections we knew that, as with album designs, DVD packaging could range from extravagant to no expense spent. We wanted our DVD to reflect the love and thought that was going into making the film, without getting into excessive cost. We also had to consider that the weight of the thing would impact on postage costs, when we got as far as actually selling it.

What should be on the DVD, apart from the film? And how should it be presented? We heard the word 'authoring' for the first time. Which is essentially the process of preparing and organising all the material that's going onto the disc – creating artwork and user menus, inserting chapter points, adding any overdubs and commentaries or special features, setting autoplay and/or repeat options, etc. This involves technology and expertise that was way beyond our capabilities, so whoever was producing the DVD for us would need to do all that too.

We also found out that there's a limit to how much material can be contained on a standard DVD – around 120 minutes of video with stereo sound. Any more than that and you have to go to a dual layer DVD which is, of course, more expensive. We knew that the film was going to run close to two hours long, and we wanted to have a few bonus features, to reward buyers and make it more attractive, so dual layer it would have to be.

Of the people that we spoke with, a company called Key Production came with the strongest endorsement. And Lisa, the lady I spoke with at Key, seemed both knowledgeable and enthusiastic. The quote they gave was competitive too, so they got the vote. We never regretted it for a moment. Over the next year Lisa would guide us through the different stages of the production process and assist our decision making with infinite patience.

By the looks of things, Key Production are still going strong and the lovely Lisa is still there. If you ever need help with putting out an album or a film, we can't recommend them (and her) highly enough.

One part of the DVD production that we were happy to do ourselves – in fact, insisted on doing ourselves – was the package design. We had some strong ideas about how it should look and, as with the Four Suns logo, I had friends from my life in advertising who could help us realise them. Andy Mawson had his arm gently and successfully twisted yet again, and we were also fortunate to be able to bring in another wonderful designer, Cristina Fernández Via, who I'd done a lot of work with while freelancing for Canon. She was to be an essential part of the operation, as she had access to the latest digital design software, which was no longer available to Andy in his seaside art gallery. It would have been infinitely harder to deliver the artwork to Key Production, in an acceptable format, without her.

We gave Andy and Cris what was hopefully a clear brief, along with the images and text that we wanted to use, and between them they did a fabulous job of capturing what we felt was the mood of the film. If you put it alongside most other DVDs – even ones that presumably had much higher production budgets – I think it's fair to suggest it doesn't just stand up but stands out. We've had many compliments about it, and I can safely say that it's the one element of the whole project that I wouldn't change in any way.

Jack - I remember you sent me the artwork and I thought it looked pretty good. I hadn't even considered that. I didn't know what we were going to do about that. I didn't know you had some mates who would be able to put it together. But I remember you emailing over the artwork and thinking "Wow, that looks pretty good. That looks professional."

We'd decided early on that, rather than having the standard plastic case, with the artwork printed on paper and slipped in, we would have it made from card, with the printing done directly onto it. We'd seen plenty of other designs using this approach and, from the many options available, we went for a four panel Delgapack (I'd never heard of it either) on grey card. This would cost a bit more and, when the printers saw our dark, largely monochrome artwork, they were concerned about how well it would come out on grey card. But we were told that we would be able to switch to white card, if necessary, after seeing a test run.

The three of us went down to the printing plant in Kent and, when it came off the presses, we were very happy with the way it looked. It came out much better than the printers expected. But there was to be, literally, another twist.

Jack - When the printers showed us how it was going to be, I asked if they could flip it over, so the rough side of the cardboard, which was supposed to be on the inside, was on the outside. Because that was how the 'There Will Be Blood' packaging was done.

The printers clearly thought we were a bit mad, but they gave it a go and, to everyone's delight, it looked even better. Even more distinctive and with a final touch of class and authenticity. We signed it off and came away with the test sheet to show off, along with a feeling that what we'd been working on for more than two years was now becoming very real.

We'd opted for a print run of 5000, which we hoped would be a sensible balance between getting a lower unit cost and a not totally unrealistic estimation of what we might actually be able to sell. For a small extra charge we got this split into two halves, so we wouldn't be filling the house with boxes all in one hit. I think Lisa, who had infinitely more experience of producing CDs and DVDs, for many different artists and companies, felt we were being overly ambitious with our order. She was certainly surprised when, having taken delivery of the first consignment on 25th October 2013, we were calling for the second batch less than two months later.

DVD packaging, by Andy Mawson and Cristina Fernández Via.

Selling the DVD

Since all our efforts to find a distributor for the DVD had come to nothing, we set about promoting and selling it ourselves. It was either that or severely test Tricia's patience by having the house cluttered up for a prolonged period while we waited, probably in vain, for a white knight.

Our marketing strategy, if you could call it that, had two main prongs. The guys at Start Productions had recommended a gentleman called Jon Mills. At the time he was (and still is) running a magazine called *Shindig*, which was similar in many ways to *Zigzag*, at the time I was involved. He also had a PR agency called, auspiciously, No Other. Their website described themselves as 'A small London based company who represent new bands, artists and book publishers'. It also said they specialised in projects "that put the music first and worry about sales afterwards". It sounded like a perfect fit.

When we met up with Jon he was, as his agency name suggested, a huge Gene Clark fan, and he was eager to get involved. So we agreed that he would take care of the media side of things, drumming up reviews and other coverage of the DVD's release. He had contacts that we didn't have and would be likely to get listened to, when we probably wouldn't. As the 'Reviews' section of this book shows, he did a pretty good job. And the fee he charged probably wouldn't have covered the weekly florist's bill for a more traditional PR outfit.

Our other avenue of promotion was through social media – a channel which was becoming more used and more important with every passing year. This had three supreme virtues, so far as we were concerned. It allowed us to reach the people most likely to be attracted to our film, through specific interest groups; it had a global coverage; and it was free.

We created a basic website, containing some information about the film, some clips from it and (most importantly) a shop page. We started a Paypal account for taking orders. And we set up a Facebook page and Twitter account. We also joined numerous other Facebook pages that had a special interest in the artists and musical genres that would include or be relevant to Gene Clark and The Byrds. In yet another fit of optimism we rented a franking machine, to make postage cheaper and easier, and we were ready to take on the world.

As soon as we put up posts announcing the release of the film on all those Facebook sites, with the link to the Four Suns website, orders started coming in – from fans, from record stores and from wholesalers – and our own Facebook page started accumulating hundreds of followers, who proved to be invaluable in spreading the word further.

We didn't want to stretch people's good will by overdoing the social media messages. But whenever there was something of interest to put up – news about the BBC broadcasts, for example, or links to reviews and interviews – we would do it. And later on, when orders started to flag, we would do occasional paid-for marketing campaigns on Facebook. These could be targeted with considerable demographic precision, they only cost a few dollars and they always produced a spike in sales.

After the first flush of orders, the monthly cost of hiring the franking machine started to outweigh the savings on postage and the added convenience, so that went back to the suppliers. Thereafter I became a very familiar face at our local post office.

Uncut magazine's 'Best Music DVDs of 2013' list. It was nice to be included… even if they got our name wrong!

PREMIERES ETC

Film festival screenings were off the table, at least for the foreseeable future, because of the cost of licensing all the music and archive material for theatrical release. But we still wanted to show the film in public, if only so more people could see it, we could thank the people who'd help us make it and we could get a feeling for how they reacted to it in the moment.

London

To anticipate the release of the DVD at the end of October 2013, we decided to have a screening somewhere in London. Partly to get attention from the media and partly to thank all those (at least, all those in the UK) who had helped and supported us along the way.

We researched a whole range of possibilities, most of which were ruled out either by cost or unavailability, before alighting on The Roxy Bar & Screen, an establishment just south of the river close to The Shard, described by *Urban Life* magazine as "probably the coolest cinema venue in London, if not the UK". After an exchange of messages established that price and availability were in the zone, we went to check it out.

It felt like a very laid-back place. A long bar at the street end led through to the screening room, which was more like a large living room, with a random selection of armchairs, sofas and tables facing a screen about the size of one of the smaller ones in a multiplex. We were assured it would hold 100-150 people without being overcrowded. After a brief pow-wow over a beer, we agreed it was perfect.

Hiring the whole joint for a Sunday afternoon was the cheapest option (unsurprisingly it was usually used for events or open to customers in the evenings), and that also seemed like the best time to attract the array of friends, family and media folk who we wanted to invite. The afternoon of October 13th was free, just before we were due to take delivery of the DVDs and start distributing them, so we grabbed it. As my birthday is on June 13th, I've never thought of 13 as an unlucky number.

Our list of invitees lengthened significantly, as people we invited asked if they could bring others. We didn't want to refuse, even though we became a bit worried that we might be overfilling the place. Which was an unnecessary concern. On the day, despite all but a handful of the expected crowd showing up, it was fine. In fact, it was a fabulous afternoon.

We had plenty of time, so we didn't rush things, allowing full use of the bar to let people get acquainted or re-acquainted and in the mood. The screening ended up being delayed by about half an hour beyond our original schedule, however, as the link between the laptop with the film on it and the Roxy's projection system didn't work as expected – or as it had worked with no problems when we did our recce. The two guys who were on duty at the club couldn't fix it, so had to summon their manager. Fortunately he wasn't far away and soon got things running. In the interim, not for the first time, Sid Griffin stepped up to the plate and entertained the assembled company with tales and reminiscences of his time with Gene Clark. It wasn't planned and he had to extemporise brilliantly, but it was actually the perfect set up.

Watching the audience watching the film that we'd spent two years making was a fascinating experience, as I wandered round the perimeter of the room, observing from different vantage points. They seemed to be fully engaged (no-one walked out!), laughed at the right moments and at the end, when the lights went up, I could see several moist eyes being dried.

As people reconvened back at the bar, we were subject to a deluge of compliments and congratulations. I was especially gratified to have really positive feedback from friends of Dan and Jack, who were much

younger than most of the audience and had never heard of Gene Clark.
Apparently several of them bought albums as a result of seeing the film.
Another unexpected outcome was an invitation to go on a London radio
show a few days later – the first of several radio appearances, some
done in person and some via transatlantic phone lines.

*Dan - I'm always a bit cynical about my own stuff, so I probably
imagined people were going to think it was a bit shit. But they didn't.
And I watched it again with friends, when it was on the BBC. But seeing
your own stuff, you notice things that piss you off. I don't think it looked
rubbish. That's not what I'm saying. I'm just saying the lighting could
have been a lot better. But we worked with what we had in the budget
and the equipment we had. And we made it work.*

Los Angeles

We had a couple of invitations to do film festivals in California, as soon
as word about the film started to spread, but we hadn't been able to
work out a way of doing it without getting (paying for!) theatrical
release licences that we couldn't afford. Taking a chance on staying
under the radar and just doing it, so close to the home town of the film
and record companies who owned most of the rights, would have felt
pretty reckless.

But out of the blue, in late 2013 just after the DVD had come out, I got
an email from a gentleman who organised arts events of various kinds
at the South Pasadena Public Library – everything from film screenings
and live performances to art exhibitions and poetry readings. He was
yet another Gene Clark fan and wanted to know if he could show the
film in their theatre, perhaps prefaced by some live music, as part of
their programme of community events.

After an exchange of messages, it became clear that this offer was
particularly attractive because a) admission would be free, b) we could
invite as many people as we liked, and c) the organisers would give me

an honorarium (a fee), if I was able to be there in person, to present the film and do a Q&A, along with complimentary accommodation for the night at a local inn.

Since Tricia and I were planning to do a California road trip in 2014 anyway, this was clearly too good an opportunity to pass up. A date was arranged for September 18th and we started putting the rest of our schedule together around it, which included a screening in…

Mendocino

Although it's small and out of the way, Mendocino was a focal point of the film and a significant percentage of our shooting for it was done there. So I'd always liked the idea of going back there to show the film in the company of Gene's family and friends who still lived in the area, as well as other locals who had known him. It would also mean showing Tricia a particularly lovely part of the world.

While doing the shoot, I'd met up with a lady who was active in the town's music and arts scene, so I got in touch with her again, to ask for suggestions about the best way of organising such an event. To my great delight, she not only had suggestions but was happy to put them into practice on our behalf. She found a suitable venue – Hill House, a handsome old inn on the outskirts of town with a good sized events room – and booked it for Saturday 13th September. In addition to showing the film, there would be live music with a band, including Kai Clark and Jon Faurot, playing Gene Clark songs.

The two events couldn't have been more different. The Mendocino one was very rustic and became increasingly rambunctious as the evening progressed and the bar did a roaring trade. And the antiquated equipment provided for the screening was far from being state of the art, so the look and sound fell some way short of perfection. But it didn't seem to affect audience reaction. Several members of the Clark family flew in from Kansas City for the occasion, other friends came from far and wide, and lots of acquaintances were renewed after many years. Tears flowed, both during the screening and afterwards, as folk circulated. This wasn't what I'd planned for, when making the film, but it was touching to witness.

The Pasadena show, in the elegant surroundings of the historic (at least by American standards) library theatre, was rather more sedate. But it also became a forum for the renewal of old friendships. Kelly Clark made a rare excursion out of San Francisco to join us, which felt like a real stamp of approval, and I was particularly pleased to be able to seat Leland Sklar and Mike Utley together – despite their many years as core members of the LA session musicians community, it turned out (to my astonishment) that they hadn't seen each other since working on the 'No Other' album forty years earlier.

The music in Pasadena, which came before the film was shown, was supposed to feature Carla Olson doing Gene Clark songs accompanied by David Plenn, a notable local guitarist. The line-up expanded as the set progressed, however, and was almost derailed when Pat Robinson joined them, in an advanced state of refreshment. After the live music ended and things had settled down, I introduced the film. But the planned Q&A never happened. As soon as the credits had finished rolling, the theatre emptied in a mass rush to the loos, which I guess is what happens when a middle-aged audience has been sitting for two hours without a comfort break. I still got my honorarium, though, along with loads of enthusiastic comments when people returned from the rest room, so it felt like the evening was a success.

Not only, but also…

As things turned out, there were a fair few more public screenings over the next couple of years, in several different countries. Either at small festivals or at events organised by Gene Clark fans.

We got round the licensing issue in one of two ways. In cases where the event was raising money for a charity, the tickets were free in exchange for a donation to the charity. And in others, the audience bought tickets to see something else – usually a live performance – with the showing of the film as a bonus.

One other thing that gave us an outlet to public awareness came in early 2014. Among Gene's younger generation of fans were the duo from Beach House, an American indie band who had been enjoying a notable degree of success in recent years. They'd decided to get together with mates from other bands, including Fleet Foxes and Grizzly Bear, to do a special tour celebrating the 'No Other' album, which they said they were "infatuated by".

The manager of Beach House got in touch when they were planning the tour, to ask if they could show our film to introduce the live performance. Expecting an audience to sit (or rather, stand) through a two hour documentary, when they'd come to see a band, seemed a bit too demanding. So it was decided to use a much shorter edit, focused on the chapter of the film that covered the 'No Other' album.

They ended up doing a short run of dates around cities in the north-eastern corner of the States, then came over to play at the End Of The Road festival in the UK in the summer of 2014. Sadly I missed that, as we were away at the time. Folk who did get to see the show, however, said it was fantastic and The Guardian described it as "an extraordinary display of talent". Clips on YouTube suggest that they did indeed do an amazing job of reproducing the record in all its multi-faceted glory. (Just put 'No Other Band' into the YouTube search box. I'm sure you'll be as blown away as I was.)

The downside was that we couldn't get any income from any of these screenings around the world, as that would have risked unwelcome attention from the corporations who owned the rights to the music. In fact we always had a modest outgoing, as we had to send a screener to the people organising the events. The upside, apart from the satisfaction of knowing that the film was being seen and getting some nice feedback, was that hopefully we were getting some extra DVD sales as a result.

The last hurrah

Once the pandemic and lockdown hit, of course, the invitations to do screenings came to an abrupt end, along with the rest of normal life as we know it. Then in September 2022, quite out of the blue, I got an email from a gentleman in Norway, who was helping to organise a festival of music films in Halden, about an hour south of Oslo. Apparently Norway's leading music critic had been asked to choose one of the films to be shown at the festival, and he'd asked for 'The Byrd Who Flew Alone'.

Once I'd been reassured that there would be free admission to the screening, I was only to happy to agree to the proposal. Especially as it came with an invitation to make an all expenses paid appearance at the festival, to introduce the film and do a Q&A.

I have to say, late February probably isn't the ideal time to be visiting the backwoods of Norway. But it was great to see the film with an audience again. And, as a big added bonus, it was shown in Halden's very new, very well equipped cinema complex. I'd never seen it look or sound as good. And the comparison I was able to make, with a couple of other films that were being shown, suggested that we'd done bloody well on the technical side of things, even with the limitations we were working under. Conversations with other film makers who were there proved I wasn't the only one to be impressed.

If 'The Byrd Who Flew Alone' never gets shown in public again, it went out on a high.

With Kai Clark at the Mendocino screening.

With Rick Clark at the Mendocino screening.

With Kelly Clark at the Pasadena screening.

Lee Sklar, Tom Slocum and Kelly Clark at the Pasadena screening.

With Johnny Rogan RIP at the Roxy screening in London.

On the red carpet at the Halden International Music Film Festival.

THE REVIEWS

In the weeks following the release of the DVD, we got a whole host of reviews and other media coverage around the world – online and in hard copy publications. Some of which came from complimentary copies that the PR company had sent out, but many of which were written by reviewers who had actually bought it. All were positive. Some very much so. Here are a few examples.

Uncut magazine

DVD & Blu-ray

SCORING
10 A true classic 9 Essential 8 Excellent
7 Very good 6 Good 4-5 Mediocre 1-3 Poor

THIS MONTH: STONES IN HYDE PARK | PECKINPAH | WALTER HILL

No underachiever: Gene Clark in the 1970s

GENE CLARK
The Byrd Who Flew Alone

FOUR SUN PRODUCTIONS

A dark chronicle of his life and works. *By Andrew Mueller*

8/10

FOR ALL THAT Gene Clark's story is as peculiar as its wilful, idiosyncratic and volatile subject, it is also one of the most trodden trajectories in modern popular mythology. "Take a group of young men," sighs one of Clark's collaborators, David Crosby, "give them some money, introduce them to drugs... I don't think there was anything wrong with the fact that we all of a sudden got laid a lot. But the money and the drugs... that'll do it every time."

The Byrd Who Flew Alone is subtitled "The Triumphs And Tragedy Of Gene Clark". It's a straightforward chronicling of Clark's life and his works, which never quite permits itself to become a celebration of his extraordinary and resonant gifts. This is partly because of an implicit suggestion that maybe the determinedly diffident Clark could or should have done (or at least sold) more, mostly because everyone knows how this particular cautionary fable ends: dead at 46, killed by a bleeding ulcer engendered by decades of drink and drugs, topped terminally up via the windfall generated by Tom Petty covering one of his oldest songs ("I'll Feel A Whole Lot Better", an irony about as leaden as they come).

We're told how Clark grew up poor, raised along with 12 siblings on the outskirts of Kansas City in a house without indoor plumbing. He was famous before he was out of his teens, recruited from his high-school rock band by The New Christy Minstrels. He wearied, not unreasonably, of the Minstrels' wholesome folk (in the archive footage of this period, Clark is conspicuously awkward in a suit and side-parting). Arriving in Los Angeles in 1964, he wandered into the Troubadour and saw Roger McGuinn playing American folk tunes rearranged in somewhat Beatlesesque fashion. Clark joined The Byrds. He was a megastar before he was 21.

As *The Byrd Who Flew Alone* tells it, Clark spent his remaining 26 years struggling, with infrequent success, to reconcile an internal riot of contradictory instincts as he proceeded, as McGuinn recalls it, "from innocent country boy to road weary and just tired of it all". Clark was at once a purist artist and a swaggering rock star. He craved pastoral simplicity, yet spent his money on Porsches and Ferraris. He never appeared happier than when playing music, but hated touring. He treasured the independence his success paid for, but paid little attention to his finances. He wanted to be left alone, but missed the applause when it wasn't there. He was neither the first nor the last to attempt to drink, smoke, snort and shoot his way through these contradictions. Everyone who knew him speaks of him with a kind of affectionate sorrow.

Yet the music that interrupts the rueful testimonies of family, friends and colleagues sounds nothing like failure. Though *The Byrd Who Flew Alone* does a serviceable job of relating Clark's biography, it is difficult not to wish it dwelt a little less on how Clark screwed his health and life up, and a little more on the astonishing music he created despite the best efforts of his legion demons. The film – correctly – brackets Clark alongside the even more wretchedly self-destructive Gram Parsons as a godfather of modern Americana, but seems generally more intent on wringing its hands than applauding. In fairness, this is probably only to be expected when so many of the talking heads – including Clark's wife, his kids, a brother and a sister, Crosby, McGuinn and Chris Hillman – are recalling first and foremost a husband, father, sibling or friend, rather than a musician.

For those of us who weren't obliged to worry about what his work was costing him, the niggling subtext to the effect that Clark underachieved is risible. He was the principal songwriter on The Byrds' first two albums. The solo records he made in the late '60s – one with the Gosdin Brothers, two with bluegrass maestro Doug Dillard – are pretty much the lodestone of country rock, for better (The Byrds, in cahoots with Parsons, finally caught up with Clark on *Sweetheart Of The Rodeo*) and for worse (Bernie Leadon, who played bass on the Dillard albums, later joined the Eagles, and took "Train Leaves Here This Morning") with him. His 1974 album, *No Other*, is rightly described here as a classic. And the songs breathe still: Robert Plant and Alison Krauss' 2007 stunner *Raising Sand* contained two Clark compositions.

It is indisputably sad and outrageous that Gene Clark's name is not better known, but such is the fate of pathfinders in all fields: the ground they clear, often at considerable risk, ends up profitably settled by the meeker spirits who follow them. *The Byrd Who Flew Alone* is a richly merited monument, if one less succinct than Clark's actual monument, a simple gravestone in his birthplace of Tipton, Missouri, which reads "Harold Eugene Clark: No Other". Indeed.

EXTRAS: None.

Mojo magazine

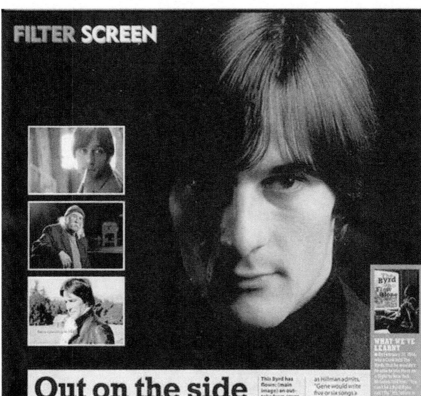

FILTER SCREEN

Caption (top left image): *Gene circa 1970s* (approximate)

WHAT WE'VE LEARNT

Caption: *The Byrd Flew Alone*

Out on the side

Saluting the heart and soul of the man who invented country rock. "Gram who?" says **Ross Bennett**

The Byrd Who Flew Alone: The Triumphs And Tragedy Of Gene Clark

★★★★

FOUR DVDs, INFO

At the beginning of this long overdue look back at the life and music of Gene Clark, his friend and fellow Byrd Chris Hillman sits back in his chair and ponders: "He sang from his heart and he had great songs… why didn't it work?" It's a question that this compelling documentary asks again and again, and one that lies at the very heart of Clark's journey from folkie to rock'n'roll star and beyond.

One of the biggest obstacles to making a film about Gene Clark is, of course, the resounding lack of Gene Clark footage, but the film-makers do an excellent job of splicing together the little there is (witness the magnificent Byrds clips and the film of Silver Raven) with warm-hearted reminiscences from all the main players in his life.

Clark's immersion in bluegrass and country began early and he cut his first record, Blue Ribbon, aged 14. Despite this, his family's hopes only ran to him becoming a country star in Nashville. Tellingly, his sister Bonnie reveals "he would have been comfortable with that life". As quickly becomes apparent, "comfort" would be a rare sensation in Gene Clark's life.

In 1963 the folk world came calling in the form of The New Christy Minstrels, but the heavy touring schedule (his chronic fear of flying started here) was enough to make him quit the group and head to Los Angeles where he met fellow folk aficionados David Crosby and Roger McGuinn.

The Byrds may have hit Number 1 with their cover of Mr Tambourine Man, but it was Clark and his prolific output of folk rock originals that would ensure the band could fill LPs. I Feel A Whole Lot Better, Set You Free This Time, Eight Miles High –

Caption (centre): This Byrd has flown: (main image) an out-take from cover shoot for 1967's Gene Clark With The Gosdin Brothers LP; (insets, from top) Clark circa '66; fellow Byrd David Crosby; Gene in 1985.

Pull-quote: "HE SANG FROM HIS HEART AND HE HAD GREAT SONGS… WHY DIDN'T IT WORK?" CHRIS HILLMAN

– as Hillman admits, "Gene would write five or six songs a week." Footage of The Byrds in their 1965 prime also attests to Clark's commanding stage presence, those inner-looking tendencies manifesting themselves in moody beatnik flourishes and a "piercing countenance" that mined the melancholy beneath McGuinn's chiming Rickenbacker.

As the band's chief songwriter he also enjoyed material success, bought a Ferrari and later began dating Michelle Phillips, the sort of rock star ostentation that rankled with the rest of the group. Clark pushed the self-destruct button (again) in early 1966, kickstarting the most fascinating decade of his life, a period that would produce three magical albums, The Fantastic Expedition Of Dillard & Clark (1968), White Light (1971) and 1974's truly extraordinary No Other.

Recurring dependencies on drugs and alcohol would pockmark his final decade with almost highs and nasty lows, but as we hear, those mystical songs of love and loss cut through the missed opportunities and thudding depressions to establish The Byrds' lost soul as one of America's great songwriters.

DVD Round-Up
by Richie Unterberger

GENE CLARK
The Byrd Who Flew Alone:
The Triumphs & Tragedy Of Gene Clark
(Four Suns Productions DVD)

Gene Clark is one of the most beloved cult figures of the 60s and 70s, albeit one who was briefly in a group that had huge hit singles, so it's hardly a surprise that there's more than enough material for a full-length documentary. The surprise is more that such a film was made, given its limited commercial prospects. But here it is, the 110 minutes put together with class, some archive footage and, most importantly, key interviews with most surviving figures who worked closely with Clark and knew him well. Starting with his Missouri upbringing (including the first airing of part of a previously uncirculated solo recording he made as a teenager, Blue Ribbons), *The Byrd Who Flew Alone* spreads its coverage evenly throughout Clark's life and career. His year and-a-half or so in the Byrds is certainly part of it, but not a dominant one, the story also encompassing his brief pre-Byrds stint with the New Christy Minstrels, Dillard & Clark, his fitful solo albums, the 1973 Byrds reunion, his brief restoration to mild commercial popularity as part of McGuinn, Clark & Hillman, and his collaborations with Carla Olson. The picture that comes across won't be a surprise to those who've followed Clark's career, but it's still an interesting one: an extremely talented singer-songwriter whose strange reticence (not to mention his aversion to touring and promotion), as well as an inability to resist the temptations of Tinseltown, made for a troubled life where commercial success was hard to sustain.

Aside from his time in the Byrds and McGuinn, Clark & Hillman, there's relatively little musical or interview archive footage of Clark (though a couple of snippets of him singing melodramatic folk revival tunes with the New Christy Minstrels are prime rarities, as are some silent bits of mid-60s informal Byrds rehearsal, the latter being outtakes from a film made by Byrds co-manager Jim Dickson). Such paucity makes constructing documentaries such as these a challenge, and much of the story is told through the directors' interviews with others. On that count they score well, especially by gaining extensive comments from all three surviving original Byrds: Roger McGuinn, David Crosby and Chris Hillman. Also on board are Barry McGuire, who sang with Clark in the New Christy Minstrels, Larry Marks, producer of some of Clark's earliest solo material and the Dillard & Clark LPs, A&M Records co-founder Jerry Moss, Dillard & Clark bassist David Jackson, Carla Olson, oldest sister Bonnie Clark, youngest brother David Clark, wife Carlie, and both of his sons. Numerous less celebrated friends, back-up musicians and management / production guys also weigh in with their perspectives.

Sure, some key figures are missing, sometimes because they're no longer alive: Michael Clarke, Doug Dillard, early Byrds co-manager Jim Dickson, early Byrds producer Terry Melcher, David Geffen, and *No Other* producer Thomas Jefferson Kaye (the latter represented by some vintage lo-fi audio-only interview comments). But in combination with available archive material, it's enough to paint a pretty full portrait of a guy who was extremely creative and ambitious artistically, but lacked self-confidence on the professional fronts necessary to maintain a high profile in the music business. Fear of success, reluctance to engage in the glad-handing needed to gain and maintain stardom, a weakness for alcohol – all are factors that come up repeatedly. At times, his aversion to glad-handing amounted to shooting himself in the foot, as when he got in a fight with Asylum Records chief David Geffen, or arrived late and drunk to a meeting with RSO Records' Al Coury, whom he mocked for looking like Sonny Bono.

There's also analysis of Gene Clark the musician, not just Gene Clark the person. "One of the reasons the music was good is he didn't know the rules, at all," observes Crosby (who speaks in an oddly deliberate, drawn-out manner that falls just short of getting irritating) of the early Byrds. "We were as strange a band as I could have imagined, because there are no five more different human beings than I could possibly devise." However, speculation that Crosby undermined Clark's confidence by lobbying for Gene to play tambourine rather than guitar – reported upon at length in more than one book – is strangely unaddressed. Crosby does own up to not doing his best on the band's hugely disappointing reunion album, though: "I completely screwed it up." McGuinn's view on the reunion LP? "It was a party more than a recording session."

As to how and why he left the Byrds in 1966, things aren't exactly made clear, perhaps because they were mysterious even at the time. Fear of flight was certainly a factor. McGuinn remembers telling him "Gene, you can't be a Byrd if you can't fly"; if that was meant as a semi-joke then or now, the humour falls pretty flat. His far higher royalty earnings (as their primary songwriter at the outset) are mentioned, though it's only hinted that jealousy might have fostered resentment that made it uncomfortable for him to stick around. You have to go into the extended interview segments in the bonus features to get McGuinn's story – previously related in other sources, but still not widely known – of how Jim Dickson, seriously ill in hospital years after working with the Byrds, gave Roger a confession. He and co-manager Eddie Tickner, Dickson told McGuinn, wanted Clark to have a solo career, so they could make money off both the band and the singer-songwriter. At the time Clark left in 1966, McGuinn admits, "I'd never thought of that" as being a reason for Gene's departure, though he adds that Dickson subsequently recanted this.

As for Gene's brief time as half of Dillard & Clark in the late 1960s, David Jackson proves a loquacious interviewee. "It was just one note at a time, one line at a time, and a lot of martinis, and an interspersion of LSD," is how he, with some fondness, describes their dynamic. As for his little-commented-upon instrumental skills, in Jackson's view, for him the "guitar seemed to be only a medium. It didn't seem to be of any particular interest, other than as a medium to this melody, a support to the melody and the words." As to why Dillard & Clark ended so quickly after singer / Doug Dillard girlfriend Donna Washburn (not interviewed) entered the act, producer Larry Marks puts it plainly: "The fun kind of went out of the band."

By the early 70s Gene was married and starting a family in Mendocino, well away from the Hollywood music machine, and apparently happily so – for a while, at least. In retrospect, maybe he should have stayed there, only recording every so often, only performing on the rare occasions when he found it comfortable and convenient. A key to Clark's tragedy, though, is that while it's sometimes stated he disliked his occasional obligations to return to Hollywood and make those damned records, he wasn't exactly averse to its seedier charms once he got there. That's what his wife found when she visited during one of his extended LA stays, and learned he was living with another woman. That ended their marriage pretty quickly. "It was like I stepped out of what I thought was a fantasy, and realized in retrospect that it was insanity," she gently and regretfully states.

The last half-hour or so focuses on his post-1980 years, and, in common with the endings of many a cult rock saga, it's something of a downer. Gene was reduced to feeding his kids a constant diet of brown rice when they visited one summer, and toured as part of a reunited 'Byrds' just this side of bogus (Michael Clarke and John York being

the only other guys who'd played in the band in the 60s). A royalty windfall from a Tom Petty cover in the late 80s might have done more harm than good, greasing the way for some indulgences that exacerbated the health and alcohol problems that led to his death in 1991, aged just 46.

As the directors readily note in their commentary, there are gaps in *The Byrd Who Flew Alone* that are covered in other sources, like John Einarson's fine Clark biography *Mr. Tambourine Man* and Johnny Rogan's mammoth *Byrds: Requiem For The Timeless* book. Though the 110-minute length is hardly short for a documentary, it's understandable that some projects and relationships had to be left uncovered in the limited time available. Still, it's unfortunate that his brief attempt to lead a band (the unimaginatively named Gene Clark Group) right after leaving the Byrds is not mentioned. More seriously, his role as the prime composer of Eight Miles High (co-credited to McGuinn and Hillman) is not discussed, though Olson points this out in one of the interview extras. His brief, disastrous return to the Byrds in late 1967 (of which some footage even exists) and solo recordings he made post-Byrds / pre-Dillard & Clark are also not remarked upon, and his affair with Michelle Phillips (not interviewed, perhaps unsurprisingly) is only noted in passing.

As compensation, you do get an entertaining story of Joe Cocker interrupting a *No Other* session by yelling down the talkback button. More unexpected is David Clark's citation of this John Fogerty quote (in the extended interview extras): "If Dillard & Clark had been more hungry at the time, Creedence

wouldn't have had a chance. They were that good." If any
readers can pin down the source of this remark, I'd like to
know. It just seems bizarre, frankly, and not just because Dillard
& Clark and Creedence weren't that similar. By the time Dillard
& Clark's first LP came out in late 1968, CCR (whose debut
had appeared several months previously) were well on their way
to success, and not likely to be worried about a country-rock
act with far less overt commercial appeal. Or was Fogerty just
trying to be nice – though he's never been known as the nicest
or most charitable fella? (Producer / co-director Paul Kendall
does note it's possible Fogerty said it to David Clark in person,
as David hung around with Gene for a while in L.A. in the late
60s, during which he met some of his older brother's famous
acquaintances.) You'll have to dig into the commentary to find
another piece of trivia of interest to hardcore Clark fans. It's
sometimes been reported that his fear of flying stemmed from
witnessing a plane crash when he was growing up in Kansas;
Paul Kendall found that there were actually no plane crashes in
the Kansas City area at the time, concluding that it's probably
an urban legend.

Other extras include a couple of inessential performances
of Silver Raven – one a black-and-white solo clip from an
unidentified date (though it seems to have been filmed not long
before Clark's death), the other in shaky, grainy color from a
1987 full-band performance. This DVD is worth finding even
if you saw the principal feature at a film festival or some such
event, as it adds almost an hour of additional interviews and a
directors' commentary. The latter, by Paul Kendall, co-director

Jack Kendall and director of photography Dan Kendall,
usefully points out the sources of some of the more unusual
archive material and stories behind how some of the interviews
were conducted and arranged (though unfortunately Dan's
voice is poorly miked).

Richie Unterberger spoke to Paul Kendall about the making of The Byrd Who Flew Alone

**You've been a fan of Gene Clark for many years, and
even interviewed him when he was in the UK in the
mid-70s. What was the motivation to produce and
co-direct a documentary about him?**
There were two primary motivations – one altruistic and one
personal. As a long-time fan of Gene's music, I was increasingly
frustrated by the unfairness of his lack of recognition and
respect – especially in comparison with Gram Parsons (whom
I also like a great deal, by the way). When I saw *Fallen Angel*,
the Gram doc that came out a few years ago, I thought Gene
deserved the same treatment. I'd been vaguely looking around
for a suitable project, and when I found out that (although
there had been several proposals for such a film over the years)
none of them had come to anything, I thought maybe the
fickle finger of fate was pointing at me. Which brings us on
to the personal motivation. I'd reached the point in my life
where I no longer wanted or (more crucially) needed to do a

Paul Kendall with Gene's son Kelly at a screening of the movie

full-time job. But I wasn't ready for golf and gardening, so I
was on the lookout for a project that would keep me out of
mischief – ideally something that would combine my first love,
music, with my interest and enjoyment of filmmaking. Two
of my sons were embarking on careers in filmmaking and
photography, so that also felt like a good way of giving them
some valuable experience.

**What experience did you bring to the documentary
in terms of background in filmmaking and /
or journalism?**
Over a 30-year career as an advertising copywriter, I'd been
involved with a lot of films, from 30-second commercials
to much longer corporate stuff, so I had a good working
knowledge of many aspects of the film-making process...
though not all! I'd also been a music writer in my 20s, mostly
for *ZigZag*, and still had some useful contacts from those days.
Jack and Dan, my two sons, brought technical knowledge and
particular skills in editing and cinematography to the table.
Having said that, it was a steep learning curve for all three of us.

**Obviously you weren't able to interview everyone
who had an important role in Gene's life and career,
especially as some of them have died. Who were
the figures you most regretted not being able to
interview (dead or alive)?**
Thomas Jefferson Kaye – perhaps the most influential of
Gene's several great collaborators. It would have been great
to get his take on Gene's talent. Jim Dickson – who was very
ill when we started on the project and passed away before

we got as far as shooting anything. Michael Clarke – the original Byrd with whom Gene had the closest personal relationship, and who worked with him across the span of their careers. Bernie Leadon [who played with Dillard & Clark] – was going to give us an interview, but changed his mind. He said he hadn't enjoyed contributing to the Gram Parsons doc, talking about an old friend with a sad story and tragic end, and didn't feel inclined to repeat the experience with Gene. Doug Dillard – we had hoped to visit Nashville, on our way back from California, to do interviews with Doug and Bernie. I spoke with Doug a couple of times on the phone and he was clearly very unwell, so there was some doubt about whether he would be able to do an interview. When Bernie dropped out, we reluctantly decided we couldn't risk spending a sizeable chunk of our minimal budget going to Nashville on the off-chance that Doug would be up to it. He died a few months later. Jesse Ed Davis – *White Light* is probably my favourite Gene album (certainly the one I play most often). I would have liked a first-hand account of its creation. Chris Ethridge [bassist] – in the absence of Gene and Jesse Ed, he may have been the next best source of information about *White Light*. We did get in touch, but he was living in Mississippi and, like Doug, was very ill. So, sadly, we had to make that same tough decision re. use of budget. Tom Petty – again, we thought that was going to work out, but he became unavailable shortly before we flew to LA. There was no explanation, but I wondered if there's some sensitivity around the 'death by royalties' issue, as it was the windfall from Tom's version of Feel A Whole Lot Better that funded Gene's fatal return to bad habits.

You already knew a great deal about Gene from having read the John Einarson biography and Johnny Rogan's Byrds tome, but what were the biggest surprises to you in what you found out in the course of making the documentary?
As you know, the Einarson and Rogan books don't leave many stones unturned, so there wasn't much that came as a surprise. The one piece of information that was completely new to me was about Gene's father, Kelly. It's well known that he was a keen musician who was Gene's first teacher and influence. But, according to Gene's brother David, he was good enough to have been offered a job with Gene Krupa. He had to turn it down, though, as he was about to get married and his wife-to-be didn't want him wandering off on tour. On such moments, history turns!

One of the most interesting finds for Clark fans will be the use of his early recording Blue Ribbons on the soundtrack when discussing his adolescence. How did you gain access to this and get permission to use it?
[Gene's son] Kai Clark has a cassette of the recording, which was recovered from the house in Sherman Oaks where Gene died. He very kindly gave us permission to make use of it. We'd spent some time with Kai up in Mendocino, when we did the interview with him, and I think he'd decided we were worthy of his trust. We weren't allowed to use the complete song, though. We wouldn't have wanted to do that in the film, anyway, but I'm sure fans would have liked it as one of the bonus features.

There are a couple of snippets of Gene singing passages of folk revival songs with the New Christy Minstrels on Hootenanny. How did you become aware of and find these?
The NCM clips are on YouTube, so they were easy to find. But tracking down the rights owners and decent reference of them took a bit longer. Apparently ABC destroyed the original videotapes (!), so what bits of the show that still exist are only on kinescope copies, which is why the quality is a bit ropey.

Were Crosby and the other Byrds reluctant to discuss sensitive matters (like division of songwriting credits) that might have contributed to Gene's lack of confidence and departure from the Byrds?
When we interviewed Crosby and (particularly) McGuinn, we were clearly on sensitive ground when we tried to discuss Gene's departure from the Byrds. They were both happy to trot out the party line re. the final plane trip [where an anxious Clark got off a plane before it took off in early 1966, leaving the band shortly afterwards], but they didn't want to explore other reasons for the fallout or their relationships with Gene. The predominant vibe from Crosby was regret and mystification, while McGuinn felt like he was talking about the black sheep of the family, with a mixture of disapproval and embarrassment. Chris Hillman was slightly guarded – I sensed he didn't want to say anything that would upset Crosby or McGuinn – but generally far more open. On a more general note, we didn't want the film to be too focused on the Byrds. Although that's the most celebrated episode in Gene's career, it's only one episode, which has been well documented elsewhere. We wanted to show what he did, with that band, in the much wider context of his life and work as a whole.

Aside from his stints with the Byrds and McGuinn, Clark & Hillman, there's relatively little Gene Clark archive footage from which to draw. Was this a challenge to you in constructing the documentary?
"Relatively little" is an understatement! Between leaving the Byrds and hooking up with MCH, there is literally no footage of Gene, apart from an appearance on *The Dating Game* with the other members of the Gene Clark Group. But we knew that going in, and decided to compensate by shooting as much location footage as we could, in Missouri, LA and Mendocino – the three key places in his life. It always seemed to me that Gene's immediate surroundings were more important in influencing his mood and work than whatever was going on in the wider world, so we wanted to give a strong sense of those places.

It seems that Gene had the opportunity to lead a happy life with his family in the early 1970s in Mendocino, yet something drew him back to a more troubled path. Do you have any speculation as to why he didn't stay in Mendocino, recording and performing when it suited him, and perhaps then still being alive with a supportive family today?
I'm not a psychologist, so I wouldn't presume to speculate on Gene's state of mind and the issues that he seems

to have wrestled with throughout his life. But we know that, even while he was based in Mendocino, he divided his time between that rural existence and regular returns to the hubbub of LA. And several of the people who we interviewed referred to the fact that he was torn between those very different worlds. His roots, personal and musical, were in the peace and stability of the country, but he was also drawn to the spotlight, and relished some of the rewards that came with it. Sadly for him, and for those closest to him, he was never able to rationalise the two sides of his story.

In the commentary track you mention that you interviewed Gene for ZigZag. Did that interview actually get printed, and if so, in which issue?
It was in the June 1977 issue.

I know it was just once, but what were your impressions of Gene from having met and talked with him? In the documentary, you say that he and Lowell George were among the most memorable of the artists you interviewed.
It wasn't so much that Gene and Lowell were more interesting than some of the other artists I interviewed – many of them were very interesting – but that they felt like people you could interact with on an equal footing... guys you could just have a beer and a chat with. Which is exactly what I did with Gene. I remember him as a very unstarlike star – quite shy, vulnerable, soulful and somewhat naïve (in the sense of being unworldly, rather than dumb). What struck me most was that, once I'd switched off the tape recorder, he genuinely seemed as interested in me and my thoughts as I was in his, which isn't the usual relationship between a young nobody and a thirtysomething celeb.

What's the reaction been like so far from people who have seen the film, both from the people you interviewed and from fans?
The reaction generally has been amazingly positive – from reviewers and from fans who've taken the trouble to get in touch. But, most importantly to us, his family and friends seem to share the belief that we did justice to Gene and his music, and told his story honestly.

Are there any other documentary projects you're considering?
We've got a few ideas, some about music and some not. But the whole climate for filmmakers (and musicians) these days is so unconducive, in terms of making the work economically viable, that I honestly don't know what the future holds. Hopefully we'll get something else off the ground, though. It would be a shame not to make further use of everything we learned doing this film. ☞

Paste magazine

The Byrd Who Flew Alone: The Triumphs and Tragedy of Gene Clark

By John Rhett Thomas and Tom Sandford

Mention Gene Clark as one of your favorite musicians and almost invariably the response will be a raised eyebrow followed by the words "Gene *who*?" Namechecking alone won't cut it. Mentioning that he was a founding member of the Byrds might trigger a vague memory, but many still won't be able to actually place him, or any of his songs. And yet David Crosby's post-Byrds mega-fame with CSN, and Roger McGuinn's iconic 12-string Rickenbacker & granny glasses (vis-a-vis Dylan's "Mr. Tambourine Man" in particular) have pretty much guaranteed their admittedly rightful places in our collective cultural memory. Meanwhile, Gene Clark, a uniquely gifted songwriter who played a pivotal role in the rise of folk rock, psychedelia and country rock, but who could never seem to catch a break, has seemingly disappeared into the past.

How did this happen? Well, that's a long, sad story in itself. For Gene Clark's small but fiercely loyal cult of fans, carrying his torch through the decades has largely amounted to a silent crusade. But thanks to a long overdue critical re-evaluation, reinforcements are on the way. Robert Plant and Alison Krauss' 2007 collection *Raising Sand* won a Grammy for Album of the Year, with two Clark compositions—"Through the Morning, Through the Night" and "Polly," a devastating, heart-rending pair of songs—anchoring the proceedings. Earlier this year, a tour was launched by an ad hoc group of indie stars from bands Beach House, Grizzly Bear, the Walkmen and Fleet Foxes—plus British folk legend and early Clark advocate Iain Matthews—performing the lost masterpiece *No Other* in its entirety to sold-out crowds on America's East Coast.

But the best entry point for new fans to discover a treasure trove of some of the best music nobody's ever heard is a new documentary, *The Byrd Who Flew Alone: The Triumphs and Tragedy of Gene Clark*. Gene Clark's life is a tale of brief early stardom, followed by a painfully slow, inexorable fall. The ill-fated Missouri-born country boy hit the peak of his fame at age 20, contributing to the band's one-two punch releases from 1965, *Mr. Tambourine Man* and *Turn! Turn! Turn!* Clark's abrupt departure from the band in early 1966, however—precipitated by anxieties within and pressures without—saw him spend the remaining 26 years of his life toiling in relative obscurity, haunted by the shadow of that early success. He would go on to record great, even brilliant, records, but commercial success eluded him, and he fell headlong into a decades-long downward spiral of substance abuse that reached its grim conclusion on May 24, 1991.

For documentary creator Paul Kendall, a former music journalist (who himself interviewed Clark in 1977), this documentary has been a labor of love, albeit one with its share of obstacles. Practically speaking, Kendall, working alongside sons Dan and Jack, had to somehow work around the unfortunate—and astonishing—fact that there is no known extant footage of Gene Clark from the immediate post-Byrds period (i.e. 1966) up until his brief tenure with the quasi-Byrds reboot, McGuinn, Clark & Hillman, in 1979. This is a significant chunk of time to cover without aid of any visuals of the principal subject, apart from stills. To compound matters, this was arguably Gene Clark's most productive period as an artist. This means that much would depend on the quality of the interviews conducted especially for the documentary. And so while each interviewee provides vital information about the enigmatic ex-Byrd, it becomes distractingly apparent that the Kendalls were grappling with budgetary constraints—the most telling manifestations of which resulted in shaky camera work and some sloppy editing.

Because the Kendalls chose a subject whose post-Byrds video legacy is only slightly more substantial than someone like Nick Drake, we're lucky that so many key individuals were available to speak about Gene, including the surviving original ex-Byrds, ex-wife Carlie, sister Bonnie, brother David, sons Kelly and Kai, Carla Olson—even David Jackson from Dillard and Clark. (A sad footnote: several of the interviewees have since passed away, including Carlie Clark and producer Larry Marks).

Of the surviving original Byrds, David Crosby, rock's ever-ebullient *enfant terrible*, provides the most interesting commentary, but to be perfectly frank, he appears tired and slow in the film. More judicious editing might have helped move things along. Roger McGuinn, still looking remarkably chipper and alert, was predictably aloof; while Chris Hillman seemed genuinely eager to speak about Clark's talent.

Elsewhere, Byrds biographer Johnny Rogan speaks to Gene's songwriting. His comments are eloquent and astute, and go well beyond the usual "Hillbilly Shakespeare" explanations of Gene's unusual gifts. One wishes there had been greater allowance for discussion of the music, but lacking the accompanying visuals would have doubtless proved difficult. A late-period video of Gene singing "Silver Raven" (from his 1974 masterpiece *No Other*) was a genuine heart-stopping surprise. In those few moments the film—on the wings of that tiny bit of footage —positively soared. But it also underscored the fact that more of Gene would have accomplished so much more than any number of talking heads. But, to be fair to the Kendalls, you can't slag the doc for not including what does not exist.

In the end, one must give kudos to Paul Kendall for not only undertaking this challenge in the first place, but for bringing it to fruition with such bravery, passion and grace. *The Byrd Who Flew Alone* is not only an extraordinary accomplishment, it is a soulful testament to Gene Clark's enduring brilliance.

Pop Culture Classics

BYRD GENE CLARK'S SAD, SOLO FLIGHT

By Paul Freeman

Gene Clark is well known for the songs he wrote during his two years with The Byrds. The memorable tunes include "I'll Feel a Whole Lot Better", "She Don't Care About Time", "Set You Free This Time" and "Eight Miles High." Lesser known, but just as stirring are the masterpieces he wrote over the following years, including "Train Leaves Here This Morning," "She Darked The Sun," "Where My Love Lies Asleep," "Tried So Hard," and "Silver Raven." Two of his songs, "Through The Morning, Through The Night" and "Polly," were covered on the 2007 album "Raising Sand," by Robert Plant and Alison Krauss.

Clark's brilliant solo albums, such as "White Light" and "No Other," failed to achieve commercial success. Collaborations with artists like the Gosdin Brothers, Bernie Leadon and Doug Dillard pioneered the country-rock genre, but didn't receive their rightful recognition.

Visually striking, the magnetic Clark was blessed with a gorgeous singing voice and a gift for combining literate, intriguing, poignant lyrics with moving, haunting melodies.

But the enigmatic artist, burdened by substance abuse, often sabotaged his own career, as when he punched music mogul David Geffen. Clark died in 1991, at age 46, his genius not fully acknowledged in his lifetime.

Paul Kendall has written and co-directed an enthralling, insightful new documentary, "The Byrd Who Flew Alone: The Triumphs and Tragedy of Gene Clark."

A couple of Kendall's acquaintances had made a fine documentary, "Love Story," about Arthur Lee and the band Love. When he attended the premiere, Kendall thought, if he could find the right story, it was something he would like to try. Gene Clark had always been one of his favorites and, after reading John Einarson's biography "Tambourine Man: The Life and Legacy of The Byrds' Gene Clark," Kendall knew the singer-songwriter's life was brimming with drama.

A U.K. music journalist in the 70s, Kendall went into advertising, where he learned about filmmaking. For this documentary, he teamed up with two of his sons, Jack (co-director, editor) and Dan (cinematographer).

They shot over 40 hours of interview footage. They did over 30 original interviews, as well as piecing together vintage audio interviews. Bonus features on the DVD version include rare Clark performances, filmmakers' commentary and additional, compelling interview segments.

Among the revealing interviewees are Barry McGuire (who was in The New Christy Minstrels with Clark); the other original Byrds, Roger McGuinn, Chris Hillman and David Crosby; Carla Olson, who sang duets with Clark later in his career; and A&M Records coowner Jerry Moss. Also offering valuable anecdotes are Clark's brother, sister, sons, former wife, friends and many of the musicians with whom he worked.

The Kendalls, traveling to the U.S, shot great footage of the places where Gene lived and worked. Because his art was influenced by his surroundings, it's important to get these glimpses of timeless Missouri, frenetic Los Angeles and tranquil Mendocino. Paul Kendall talked with PCC about the triumphs and tragedy of the fallen Byrd, Gene Clark.

POP CULTURE CLASSICS: What made you so passionate about Gene's work that you wanted to devote so much time and effort to the project? PAUL KENDALL: I'd always loved Gene Clark's music, from way back. I first came across him in Dillard & Clark, back in "68. I followed his music, when I was in my music-writing stint in the 70s, when he was over there with the K.C. Southern Band in '77. Someone bought me the John Einarson book as a gift. It reminded me what a fantastic, compelling story Gene had. I thought, 'Okay, maybe this is the story I've been looking for.' But I thought surely somebody had done it already. When it didn't look like anybody had, I took it from there.

PCC: You met Gene, when he was touring in England, what were your impressions of him at that time?

KENDALL: They'd come over here to do a series of dates in the U.K., and I'd seen him at the Hammersmith Odeon in London, which is now the Apollo. And then went to one of the cities in the north, either Liverpool or Leeds, to see another gig and to interview Gene. As it turned out, the gig was canceled.

The tour was canceled. There were problems with the promoter. So I interviewed Gene for about an hour, for a magazine called ZigZag, which was a quite popular magazine in the U.K. at the time. And, when I finished interviewing him, there was nothing else to do, the gig wasn't happening, so we just went out and had a few beers into the evening. And I always remembered him, because he was the most unstarlike man, for a guy who was a big star and, in his day, a huge star. Of all the performers I interviewed or hung out with at that time, he was the least starlike of all of them. He was quite a shy man, not really terribly self-confident at all. But I thought he had a real warmth to him. Of all the people I interviewed at that time, there were only two I felt I had connected with on a purely human level. And Gene was one of them. The other was Lowell George of Little Feat. So Gene had made quite an impression on me. And the book filled in a lot of gaps. Gene really had a roller-coaster life, very sad in many ways, but he still produced an extraordinary body of work, despite that.

PCC: What was it about his music that you found to be so magical?

KENDALL: A combination of things. I think he had a fantastic sense of melody, a really unique way with lyrics. The word 'visionary' is overused these days, by the media. But, in talking to various people about the way he wrote and where he got his inspiration from, I think the word 'visionary' can be accurately used in Gene Clark's case. He got his inspiration from somewhere even he didn't know about. That's probably one of the things he struggled with, that he had this extraordinary gift for writing and didn't know where it came from. His wife, in the film, says, it just came through him. He was almost channeling. And he struggled with that. Other songwriters, who are kind of craftsmanlike, have a greater understanding of what they are doing. They may be more fortunate, in that they know what they're working with, whereas people like Gene - he's not the only one who had this God-given gift - do often seem to struggle to come to terms with it and be able to deal with it.

PCC: Having that unique gift, a lasting influence, and some fervent fans, why do you think he's been so under-appreciated by the general public?

KENDALL: I think, in a lot of ways, he was his own worst enemy in that. After he left The Byrds, and I think one of the reasons he did leave The Byrds, was that he struggled with the various pressures of stardom and being a leading light in the music world, and thereafter, he seemed to try to avoid that sort of success again. He carried on making fantastic records, but didn't do anything to actively promote them and try to turn them into the kind of successes other people had and he might well have deserved.

PCC: In the film, it seems like some friends have contradictory perceptions of whether Gene was totally disinterested in fame or whether he consciously tried to avoid that or whether he was actually seduced by it.

KENDALL: I don't think it's so much that his friends had contradictory views. I think he was contradictory himself. He was conflicted. One part of him, from what we know, one side of him enjoyed the trappings of fame and the material things that it brought, the recognition that it brought. But then there was another side of him that shied away from that, didn't like it, found it difficult to deal with.

PCC: Gene's departure from The Byrds, there's still so much difference of opinion as to whether it was the result of the pressures or the fear of flying, or the fact that he wanted to go solo.

KENDALL: I'm not sure we'll ever get to the bottom of that. The main guys in The Byrds, who probably know better than anybody else, probably aren't going to spill the beans on that. Certainly when we were interviewing, particularly David Crosby and Roger McGuinn, they kind of toed the party line about the fear of flying. Other people think that's a bit of a red herring, really. The impression I got from what I've read and from what I know from various people, it wasn't so much a fear of flying that was the problem. It was a fear of what would happen at the other end of the flight. If they were taking a flight on tour, it meant that, when they got off the plane, there would be the pressure of audiences, media people, music business people and expectations. I think that's what he was probably afraid of, rather than the actual flight.

PCC: Do you think that's why, instead of beginning his solo career by making a very Byrds-like record, he goes with the lush, epic "Echoes" single and then his collaborations with Doug Dillard, all very different from The Byrds' hits?

KENDALL: I think, in making his music, like many artists, he followed his muse, he followed his instinct. In Gene's case, he was quite strongly influenced by the people that he worked with at different stages of his career. With Dillard & Clark, obviously, he was working with Doug Dillard, who brought an awful lot to that particular combination, not maybe as much from the compositional point of view, but certainly from the musical influences point of view. And he took Gene into, well, back into, when you consider Gene's upbringing, back to a more roots, bluegrassy sort of place. And then later on, when Gene was working with Thomas Jefferson Kaye as his producer, that took him into another place. If it felt right, Gene would go there. And if it stopped feeling right, as with the end of Dillard & Clark, and various other projects, then he would go off and do something else. It was very much a case of him following his instincts, following his muse. I don't think he did much in a sort of calculated way, certainly not in a career way.

PCC: Do you think he was aware of how revolutionary it was to bring all the traditional country influence to folk-rock?

KENDALL: I doubt it. Again, I think that roots music, bluegrass, country music were ingrained in him, he was brought up with that in Missouri. That's the music his father was doing as Gene was growing up. So that was very much in him. From talking to, particularly, David Clark, his brother, and Bonnie, his sister, he had a fairly - although his childhood wasn't rich in some respects - it was quite rich in the range of music that he was exposed to, from the down-home country music that his father was playing to the church music to almost classical stuff, obviously hearing a wide range of things on the radio, Elvis Presley onward. I think all those things just came together in him. And then came out again, without any sort of ambition or planning, in his music. It had been in there and he let it out.

PCC: You mentioned his brother and sister. There are so many remarkable interviews in your film, with family, friends and peers. How did you get them to be so relaxed and candid, as if they were talking with an old friend in their living room? They really open up.

KENDALL: I think that came out of necessity to some degree. The whole way we shot it was very low-key, very minimalist. We shot most of it on a month-long trip around America. And it was just me and my two sons in a station wagon, minimal lighting rig, very small cameras. There was no film crew, no people running around with clipboards. No big fuss. We would just turn up.

Most of the interviews were done in the people's own homes, which was what we wanted, so we had them in their own setting. We would just turn up and Jack and Dan would spend maybe half an hour, an hour tops, sorting out where we wanted to actually shoot the interview, setting up the small amount of equipment. And then we'd just sit down and have a chat with whoever it was that we were interviewing. And I think that helped enormously, the fact that it was so low-key, so unpressured. There weren't people all over the place, plugging in wires and taking notes. The experienced interviewees, the David Crosbys, the Roger McGuinns, the Chris Hillmans, were kind of disarmed by it. And certainly the people like his brother and sister and the various friends who weren't used to being in front of the camera, it helped them feel comfortable. I've done a lot of interviews, over the years, for various projects. And I always try to make it sort of a dialogue, rather than a question-and-answer. I'm trying to establish a rapport with the person I'm interviewing. And that makes it more relaxed. And all that worked well for us. A number of people have commented on the quality of the interviews. That's one of the things that helped to make the film what it is.

PCC: Were you surprised by any of the material you got from The Byrds?

KENDALL: The Byrd that I was pleasantly surprised by was Chris Hillman. I was warned by a couple of people who'd interviewed him over the years that he can be a bit prickly, if you get him on the wrong day. But he was great, very relaxed, very happy to talk. And I think he comes across fantastically well in the film. He obviously cared about Gene and appreciated his talent and was almost kind of frustrated that Gene - I'm reluctant to say didn't make the most of his talent, because in one respect, he made a fantastic amount of his talent. He left a great legacy of music. But he didn't achieve the depth of recognition that he probably deserved.

PCC: Chris has said that he doesn't understand why Gram Parsons has become such a cult figure, while Gene tends to be less discussed.

KENDALL: Well, I think Gram Parsons sort of helped himself by living fast, dying young and leaving a beautiful corpse. Gene lived long enough to have 10 years of obscurity, pretty much, before he actually passed away. I'm a great fan of Gram Parsons. He's wonderful. But if you compare the two bodies of work, I think you'd have to say that Gene's is probably the stronger.

And if you look at the chronology, Gram Parsons may be referred to as the father of country-rock, but Gene Clark's first solo record was ahead of what Gram Parsons was doing.

PCC: Hillman's fondness for Gene comes across. And Crosby and Hillman seem to have a lot of respect for him. So all the tensions among The Byrds, do you think that came out of the strong egos? Jealousies?

KENDALL: As Crosby says in the film, these were five young guys who literally went from scrapping around for money for hamburgers one minute to being number one all round the world. That puts stresses and strains on you. And clearly, that was a band that had several strong personalities. So I guess the seeds of conflict were there right from the get-go. It's difficult for any combination of personalities to survive for long, when they're under the pressures and strains of those sorts of circumstances.

PCC: The success of The Byrds, do you think that was both a blessing and a curse for Gene Clark?

KENDALL: Yes, I think you'd have to say it was. Obviously it was a blessing in the sense that it put him into the spotlight and the royalty checks that he got from it sustained him for a number of years after he'd left the band, particularly in the Mendocino years, when he was making the 'White Light' album and 'No Other.' I get the impression, from talking to Carlie (Gene's ex-wife) that he was able to have that lifestyle in Mendocino, doing that great work, because he was still getting some pretty decent money from his time in The Byrds. So it was a blessing. But, on the other hand, it was obviously something that, as Ken Mansfield (a friend from Gene's Laurel Canyon years) says in the film, it was something that Gene never really managed to extricate himself from. Forever after, he was an ex-Byrd. And, particularly because he wasn't able to achieve any really significant commercial success in his own right, it was as tag he would be stuck with for the rest of his days.

PCC: Did you find it sad that he did end up forming various incarnations of The Byrds in his later years, because that was the only way he could survive?

KENDALL: Oh, I don't see how you could possibly say anything but that, the fact that he was forced to fall back on that in order to keep himself together and to make a living. Yeah, it is sad. He was worthy of better.

PCC: What did you conclude was at the heart of his self-sabotage and self-destruction? Was this something he was born with? Or a result of his inability to deal with the circumstances of fame?

KENDALL: I'm not a psychologist, so I hesitate to hazard an opinion. But I do think it was a combination of both. From what we know of his family background, clearly, there are patterns of issues running through, cropping up. But, of course, the life he led, the way that went, the stresses and strains, that can't have helped. As his sister Bonnie said in the film, had he made a living as a musician, but at a much lower, less pressurized level, then he may well have had a longer, happier life. But it's often the way with great artists that, in order for us to enjoy the art they produced, they had to lead the lives that they led.

PCC: Do you think, if Gene hadn't been such a tortured soul, we might not have had such poetic, powerful writing from him? And that wonderfully mournful sound?

KENDALL: Yeah, I think almost certainly not. I think it's unreasonable to expect, in any sphere, not only music, to expect extraordinary work to be produced by ordinary people. It doesn't work that way.

PCC: It seems like even with all the friends and fans, and he was married for several years, there was a deep-seated loneliness in him. Did you sense that?

KENDALL: Yeah. I was talking to Sid Griffin, of The Long Ryders, who knew Gene, and I told him we were calling the film, "The Byrd That Flew Alone." He said, "That's right. Gene could be alone in a crowded room. He was perhaps the loneliest man I've ever met." So you're absolutely right.

PCC: What do you believe to be Gene's primary legacy or lasting influence?

KENDALL: His music lives on. And most of it still sounds as fresh today as when it was first made. There was a kind of supergroup of Americana artists recently put together by Beach House [including members of Fleet Foxes, Grizzly Bear and The Walkmen, plus Iain Matthews], doing a tour, reproducing Gene's "No Other" album. And it created a stir. The audience, as you might expect with those bands involved, was 90 percent quite young, probably a lot of whom had never heard of Gene Clark. But apparently the reception was fantastic. If you look on YouTube, there are some performances there. So Gene's music still has the power to attract new listeners.

PCC: Are you hoping that the film, as well, will bring new listeners into his music?

KENDALL: That was absolutely the hope for the film. It was one of the primary motivations for making the film. Gene should have been treated better, in terms of his role in music history. This was a labour of love and attempt to right that wrong, to get him a bit more of the recognition that he so richly deserves. It we can do that, then mission accomplished.

PCC: Has Gene's family let you know how they feel about the completed film?

KENDALL: We hope everyone likes it. But we particularly wanted Gene's family and nearest and dearest to feel that we'd done him justice and had done a good job. And, yeah, we've heard that they're very happy with it. They feel it's a very fair reflection, an honest, balanced view of the man and his story. They feel we've done right by him, which is just what we'd hoped to do.

"The Byrd Who Flew Alone: The Triumphs and Tragedy of Gene Clark"

Matthew Greenwald

The hindsight gained in the twenty years that have passed since Gene Clark's premature death make obvious both his musical brilliance and his secure place amongst the second half of the 20th century's most important musicians.

Though several significant CD reissues and John Einarson's fine biography "Mr. Tambourine Man" have helped burnish Clark's historical and musical legacy, this appropriately venerating documentary DVD focuses his genius with extraordinary clarity.

Through a well-balanced blend of interviews, photographs and film clips (most of which have never before been seen), the documentary's producers skillfully present Gene's dazzlingly kaleidoscopic yet tragic life in a way that graphically exposes his personal and professional foibles while never losing sight of his all too brief trailblazing musical journey.

Though little video evidence exists of his early days through his time with The New Christy Minstrels, interviews with Gene's family and with fellow musical travelers at the time, including Barry McGuire, effectively tell the story.

An audio clip of "Blue Ribbons", Clark's first real recording, provides evidence of a teenager possessed of staggering vocal and emotional depth.

The segment devoted to Gene's time with The Byrds, obviously a career cornerstone, is perhaps a bit shorter than some might like, but it is astutely produced and proportional to the entire Gene Clark story.

With great reflective insight, David Crosby, Roger McGuinn and Chris Hillman all weigh in on Gene both as a human being and of course as a singer-songwriter whose overall energy, focus and artistry were key elements in the band's exquisite yet unstable chemistry.

The absence here of The Byrds' manager Jim Dickson is unfortunate. His mentorship and guidance was an important part of Gene's career both during his time as a Byrd, and in subsequent years.

Producer and co-director Paul Kendall told Analogplanet that sadly, when the project began, Jim was quite ill and that by the time they were ready to start shooting interviews, he had passed away.

The documentary covers well The Byrds ill-fated 1973 reunion album though there is no mention of the 1970-1971 era tracks "One In A Hundred" and "She's The Kind Of Girl", both of which are considered vital pivot points in Clark's rocky solo career. Hearing them or at least having them discussed would have been useful. But this is a minor criticism of what is masterful documentary filmmaking.

Gene's late '60's/early '70's post-Byrds era was his artistic pinnacle and the documentary provides excellent coverage of his work during that time with Doug Dillard in Dillard and Clark as well as of *White Light* his Jesse Ed Davis produced second solo album.

The documentary accurately, insightfully and in great detail covers this crucial, somewhat confusing period with a most effective voiceover by musician and historian Sid Griffin.

Several session players including the legendary Lee Sklar help detail the oft-celebrated 1974 *No Other* album, with a key discovery being audio snippets from producer Thomas Jefferson Kaye.

Paul Kendall commented on the stroke of luck he had documenting this period: "When we were quite advanced with the editing, a package arrived out of the blue from Garth Beckington, who played guitar with Gene on and off during the last ten years of his life. The package he sent contained a real treasure trove of stuff from Gene's Mendocino years —a period that has left little in the way of archive material. There was the video of Gene doing a solo version of "Silver Raven", which is on the DVD, (and) we instantly recognized what a lift that stuff would give to the film. It required a total re-edit of the middle chapters, but I'm sure it was worth it."

The film covers in fairly weighty detail the latter part of Gene's odyssey and his subsequent demise, focusing always on Gene's artistry, which, despite his many self-inflicted travails and calamities, seemed to shine through (albeit sporadically).

Gene's friend and fellow-musician Tom Slocum, whose perceptive commentary is honest, powerful and mindful, is the most profound voice here from this time period.
"The Byrd Who Flew Alone" perceptively and honestly defines a misunderstood and under-appreciated craftsman. It forges in steel both Gene Clark's artistic importance and his greatness as a singer-songwriter during an era that was like "no other".

Rolling Stone

New Film Reveals the Sad Flight of the Byrds' Gene Clark

'The Byrd Who Flew Alone' tracks Clark's extraordinary gifts and tragic war with limelight.
By David Fricke

On a short, recent U.S. tour, an indie-rock superband featuring members of **Beach House, Fleet Foxes** and **Grizzly Bear** performed the whole of *No Other*, a marvelous, largely forgotten 1974 album by Gene Clark, the late singer and a founding member of the Byrds. The concert's opening act was an excerpt, about that LP, from *The Byrd Who Flew Alone* (Four Suns Productions), a quietly gripping 2013 documentary by **Jack and Paul Kendall** about Clark's extraordinary gifts and tragic, losing war with limelight.

Clark, who died in 1991, was barely there, in the telling of his own story: appearing only in still photos, disembodied voiceovers from an audio interview and tantalizing footage from a TV-studio performance of an older Clark singing *No Other*'s "Silver Raven," solo with an acoustic guitar. Everything else – anecdotes about the recording, analysis of the music, regrets over its commercial failure – was left to survivors: colleagues and admirers such as the Byrds' **David Crosby**, *No Other* bassist **Lee Sklar** and **Sid Griffin** of **the Long Ryders**.

The Rapid Ascent of a Reluctant Star

Clark passes through the rest of *The Byrd Who Flew Alone* (now available on DVD) in the same way, like a ghost with a long, iron grip on others' recollections. Born in Tipton, Missouri, in 1944, Harold Eugene Clark bloomed early, busting out of the prairie with early-Sixties folk stars the New Christy Minstrels, then co-founding the Byrds with Crosby and **Roger McGuinn** in 1964. Clark dominated the group's two 1965 albums with his prolific composing and emotionally magnetic voice but never recovered from his sudden exit in late '65, ostensibly over his fear of flying. Clark issued only four major-label solo LPs in his lifetime, the last in 1977, and refused to promote *No Other* or its predecessor, the 1971 pensive-country classic, *White Light*, with tours and press campaigns.

Clark's story has been told in depth in two books: Johnny Rogan's 1997 edition of his comprehensive Byrds history, *Timeless Flight Revisited* (Rogan House) and John Einarson's 2005 biography of the singer, *Mr. Tambourine Man* (Hal Leonard). But the Kendalls do a remarkable job of bringing Clark's genius and allure to life from the scant visual evidence he left behind: rare concert footage of a clean-cut Clark with the Christys; clips of the '65 Byrds miming to their hits on dance-party TV shows; that undated "Silver Raven" clip, included in full as a bonus feature on the DVD. In one sequence, sadly without sound, Clark is seen with the other Byrds in what looks like a backstage dressing room, clapping his hands with intense concentration as if he is teaching a rhythm to a new song. He is classic-Sixties handsome, with commanding Roman-esque features; Clark is also lost, in the best way, in his music.

A Byrd in Twilight

Much of *The Byrd Who Flew Alone* is inevitably given over to Clark's extended twilight, in the Seventies and Eighties, of false career starts, personal crisis, divorce and physically ravaging alcoholism and drug use. One sad, striking measure, not in the film, of Clark's faint, public trail after the Byrds is that he was never interviewed as a solo artist for *Rolling Stone*. The first major story about him in the magazine was my obituary, published in July, 1991.

The Kendalls treat that darkness – and Clark's periodic sparks of creative recovery, like his Eighties collaboration with singer-guitarist **Carla Olson** – with a frank care. Clark's Missouri siblings **David** and **Bonnie**, his sons **Kelly** and **Kai,** Byrds bassist **Chris Hillman** and producer-songwriter **Tom Slocum** all speak with sympathy for Clark's trials and demons. They also sound hurt and still baffled by his poor choices and surrender to the consequences, even after drastic stomach surgery in 1988.

The Byrd Who Flew Alone ends with a home video, running next to the credits, of Clark singing **Bob Dylan**'s "I Shall Be Released" with a clear, grateful resolve. The setting is humble: Clark and one of his later bands performing the song, with smiles, at a kitchen table into a boom-box recorder. But in a film in which Clark is more spectre than star, you finally see, as well as hear, the legend in everyone's memories and etched forever in those records.

I've listened to the radio...

In addition to the interviews that appeared in print, there were a fair few radio appearances, either as a threesome or just me. In a couple of cases we actually visited the stations, but mostly they were done over the phone, as they were for stations in the States. Whether they added to sales of the DVD is impossible to say, but it was enjoyable to talk about the project and bask in the warmth of approval. I think every single one of the interviews came as a result of the station having a Gene Clark fan on board, rather than any PR initiative. You can find some of them on YouTube, if you really want to hear me expounding on some of this stuff in person.

GETTING ON TV

We'd always hoped that the film would be shown on TV, somewhere and at some point. But it happened sooner than expected.

Once we had the edit to a state we were happy with, in early 2013, we asked Sid Griffin if we could show it to him. Sid was very familiar with Gene Clark's work and story, and had actually known the man. He was (is) also an experienced broadcaster and documentary consultant, so he seemed like the ideal man to give us some feedback. After more than a year immersed in the edit, we needed an outside eye to help us distinguish wood from trees.

Lucky break #12

Sid thought the film was really good. He had a few suggestions, as we'd hoped he would, but was very enthusiastic and encouraging. So enthusiastic, in fact, that he there and then called a friend called Mark Cooper and told him about it. Mark just happened to be Head of Music TV at the BBC and was billed by Sid as a huge fan of Gram Parsons and other Americana. Sid had been involved with him in the making of the Parsons documentary, 'Fallen Angel'. An appointment was made to show the film to him.

Jack - When we interviewed Sid Griffin, we didn't know how important he would be... how helpful. He became quite involved in the project after that. Another example of the lucky breaks we had with this project. There were lots of situation where, if we done something a month or two later, it would have been a different story.

The meeting with Mark went very well. He also liked the film very much and was keen for the BBC to be able to show it, seeing it as ideal for a BBC4 screening on a Friday night, when that channel always had a run of music-related programmes. He even agreed that we should be allowed to do a 90 minutes edit, rather than the 60 minutes they usually asked for, as we felt very strongly that almost halving the length of the film would ruin it, while losing twenty minutes would be achievable without a major downside. (In fact there are people, whose opinions I respect, who feel that the shorter version actually works better.)

The sum they offered us for having the film was rather less than what you might expect for ninety minutes of prime time TV with a major broadcaster, but we were reliably informed that it was the going rate at the time, for programmes that the BBC bought in, rather than commissioned. A rate which had, we were told, gone down considerably in the past ten years. A while later I met the director of another music documentary, which had also been made as a labour of love and which the BBC had bought ten years earlier. He'd got £60k for his efforts. We got £15k.

It was good to be guaranteed a slug of income, though, after all the outgoings. And, crucially, by entering into a co-production agreement, the BBC were able to cover the licensing of all the songs under their blanket agreement with the organisations that collect royalties for copyright owners. We just had to get extra licences, as appropriate, for archive footage and photos. Which made a dent in the money we were being paid by the BBC, but still left a reasonable amount to bank.

The first airing on BBC4 was initially scheduled for February 2014, but it got pushed back a couple of times to make way for things that had a particular topical relevance. It finally appeared on 14th March 2014. The viewing figures, combining when it was broadcast live and during the following week when it was available on the BBC's iPlayer streaming service, was well over 400,000. Which seemed pretty good for such a niche offering. It would certainly have been the biggest audience Gene had got, for very many years. And in the immediate aftermath of the broadcast, all of his albums shot up the Amazon UK album charts. 'No Other' actually reached No.7 in the main charts, having previously been languishing somewhere in the thirty thousands. But did we get any thanks from the record companies who we'd had to negotiate so hard with to make the thing happen? I'll leave you to guess.

The BBC were certainly pleased with the way it had gone, though, and Mark Cooper asked if we had any other ideas for films we'd like to produce. I'd always thought of myself as someone who happened to have made a film, rather than a film maker, but it was an invitation I was happy to accept. A few weeks later the three of us went up to The Television Centre in Shepherd's Bush, to discuss some ideas with Mark. Here's what we had:

Writing The Wrongs

How Nick Kent became the UK's most influential music writer, and nearly killed himself in the process. (Keith Richards, Iggy Pop, Sex Pistols, Julie Burchill)

A Connected Yankee In Britfolk's Court

The story of Joe Boyd and Witchseason Productions (Fairport, Incredible String Band, Nick Drake, John Martyn, Fotheringay, Sandy Denny, Richard Thompson)

Fully Qualified Survivor

The story, past and present, of singer/songwriter Michael Chapman.
http://www.michaelchapman.co.uk/

The Band That Reinvented The Music Business

Marillion's journey from chart-topping prog rockers to pioneers of internet usage and fan-funding.
http://marillion.com/

The Little Club That Rocked The World

The story of Friars Aylesbury. (Bowie, Genesis, Mott The Hoople, The Jam, Pete Frame etc)
http://www.aylesburyfriars.co.uk/

Without Whom

Leading musicians talk about their influences. With illustrations from the BBC archives. (Paul McCartney, Elvis Costello, Johnny Marr, Damon Albarn, PJ Harvey, Alex Turner etc)

It's All Over Now

What happens after rock stars stop being rock stars. (Eg - Paul Thomson – Roxy Music > Scuba diving instructor; Richard Coles – Communards > CofE curate; Dave Rowntree – Blur > lawyer; Paul Simenon – Clash > Painter & Greenpeace activist; Craig Logan – Bros > MD RCA Records; Alannah Currie – Thompson Twins > sculptress)

Please feel free to pinch any of those ideas. It doesn't look like we'll be using them any time soon.

Mark was kind enough to say that he would have been very happy to watch a film about any of those subjects. But he told us that there had been a reorganisation at the Beeb, which saw commissioning power given to the people in charge of specific channels, such as BBC3 or BBC4, or particular programmes, such as Arena and Storyville. All he could do now was make recommendations, and he very much doubted that any of our ideas would be greeted with great enthusiasm by those people.

It was noticeable that soon after our meeting the Friday night BBC4 schedule, which had previously been a rich source of more left field music-related programming, became far more mainstream. Artists such as Nic Jones and John Martyn disappeared from view, to be replaced by an array of films about The Stones, Queen, Bowie and other usual suspects.

We got the distinct impression that, had we been a few months later in offering a Gene Clark documentary to the BBC, we would not have been welcomed and the film wouldn't have reached the nation's TV screens. In September 2015 we approached Mark again, about the possibility of interest in a film about The Incredible String Band, hoping that wonderfully quirky combo might be sufficiently well known and well-loved to stir some interest. We got a prompt reply:

"I think there should be an ISB film, they have plenty of fans! But whether current BBC FOUR would go for such a film, I rather doubt."

In May 2019, he stepped down after 20 years as the figurehead of BBC TV's music programming. At the time of writing, BBC4 shows no sign of reverting to more adventurous, less predictable stuff.

Other channels

During the couple of years after the BBC screening, we either approached or were approached by TV companies in different countries. In some cases discussions went on for some while and what seemed to be real interest was shown. In all cases, that interest foundered yet again on the rocks of licensing costs. Unlike the BBC, smaller TV companies weren't able to take us under their wing and absorb those costs. In the few cases where we actually got as far as talking about money, the deals offered would have left us substantially out of pocket.

One route that we tried really hard to follow was 'American Masters', a highly regarded series of films on America's Public Broadcast Service (PBS) network, which has been running since the mid '80s. They'd covered the full span of artists, from musicians and writers to painters and actors. Some of them gigantic figures, such as Miles Davis and Martin Scorsese; others, such as director Richard Linklater and singer/songwriter Holly Near, perhaps less obvious subjects. We knew they made or commissioned several new films each year and thought Gene Clark might be worthy of consideration.

We made numerous attempts to contact Susan Lacy, who was running 'American Masters' up till 2014, by phone, email and snail mail. We even sent her a copy of the DVD. All without any response. When she was succeeded by a new chap, we contacted him and did get a reply, asking to view the film. We sent him a Vimeo link and never heard another word, despite chasing it up. It seems they now invariably take responsibility for their own productions, only rarely accepting them from an outside source. This was one of the few real disappointments we experienced along the way. 'American Masters' would have been a perfect vehicle for getting the film – and Gene – to a much wider audience.

We had a longer interaction with the Head of Documentaries at HBO. He actually watched the film, liked it and started to explore the possibility of them showing it. But then he dropped out, albeit graciously and apologetically, without giving a reason why.

The Byrd Who Flew Alone: The Triumphs and Tragedy of Gene Clark

Profile of Gene Clark, the talented but enigmatic former Byrds frontman who made records still regarded as classics and was one of the pioneers of folk rock and country rock.

🕐 1 hour, 29 minutes

Show more

Last on

Sun 17 Nov 2019
22:55
BBC FOUR

Still listed by the BBC, though sadly no longer available.

THE 4AD SAGA

In late 2017, just when I thought I was done with spending significant chunks of my time on stuff related to the film, we got pulled back in.

On 2nd October I got an email from a chap called Steve Webbon. He was a project consultant at 4AD, one of the UK's foremost and best respected independent record labels. They'd unexpectedly acquired the rights to Gene's 'No Other' album, apparently as part of a clear out of Warner Bros massive back catalogue, and were hoping to do a bells-and-whistles reissue.

It wasn't the sort of thing 4AD usually did, at all. Their day job was working direct with artists, most of whom aren't the kind who top the singles chart. Or, indeed, the albums chart. The likes of Pixies, Big Thief and The National. But the company's founder, Ivo Watts Russell, had a particular fondness for Gene Clark and had even covered a couple of Gene's songs – 'Strength Of Strings' and 'With Tomorrow' – on albums by his own band, This Mortal Coil. Although Ivo was no longer with 4AD and was last heard of living in the New Mexico desert, he had passed on his enthusiasm to others at the company, who were jumping at the chance to give 'No Other' the treatment they felt it deserved.

In the first instance Steve was seeking contact details for folk, such as Whin Oppice, who might be able to help with providing some archive material to accompany the reissue. Once they'd received all the master tapes and realised they were getting much more than just the album as originally issued, however, they became very excited and their ambitions expanded to include not just remastered CD and vinyl versions, but a limited edition collector's box set. This was planned to include several discs worth of previously unheard outtakes, along with a lavish book and an exclusive documentary about the album.

As a Gene Clark fan, I was a bit disappointed that the many reels of master tapes disproved the rumour (started by Gene himself) that they'd recorded other songs, which didn't make the final album and have never been heard since. What they did contain was multiple versions of the songs that are on the album, as Gene and his stellar cast of LA session musicians tried out different approaches to the material, some of which were quite unlike what was finally released at the time.

Dan and Jack already knew people at the company, as they'd done photo shoots and made videos with some of their artists, so we went up to their office in Wandsworth (or rather, the pub next to their office in Wandsworth) to discuss ideas and possibilities with Steve and his colleagues. They were really nice guys and genuine music enthusiasts, unlike too many record company execs in a world where marketeers, accountants and lawyers now hold sway. We were very happy to get involved with the project. Especially as Sid Griffin was also part of the team, responsible for sorting out all the available material, making selections and putting it together, in partnership with the illustrious engineer/producer, John Wood.

In their first flush of euphoria, they were talking about sending us back to the States to shoot interviews with other people, who had been involved in the making of the album, as well as sourcing celebrity fans, who could sing Gene's praises on camera. Robert Plant, Michael Stipe and Jack White were among a load of names suggested, by us and by 4AD.

It wasn't long before someone did the sums and calmer heads prevailed. Even with our unusually cost-efficient approach to film making, their initial ideas for the new documentary would have added up to an investment that could never be recouped. Unless demand for Gene Clark product escalated beyond anyone's wildest expectations.

What we actually did was shoot new interviews with the people responsible for the reissue: Sid and John, at the studio where they were working on all the songs Sid had chosen; the head of 4AD, who had OK'd the acquisition of the 'No Other' recordings; Steve, who was overseeing the whole project and putting together the book; and the chap who was designing all the elements of the packaging. With that and appropriate material, which we'd shot or sourced for 'The Byrd Who Flew Alone', we made a film running to just over half an hour, which we called 'The Making and Remaking of No Other'. It covered the creation of the album, back in 1974, and brought the story up to date with 4AD's recreation of it. Not quite as extravagant as what had first been envisaged, but everyone seemed very pleased with it.

The release of the album, in all its forms, was eventually scheduled (at my suggestion, I think I'm right in saying) to coincide with the 75th anniversary of Gene's birth on 17th November 1944.

4AD held a very enjoyable launch event in London, featuring a playing of the remastered album – which sounded even more stunning over a big sound system - a screening of our 'No Other' documentary and a Q&A with myself and Johnny Rogan. The last time I saw him, I'm sad to say. The pandemic put a stop to meeting in person through 2020 and he passed away, suddenly and quite unexpectedly, in February 2021.

The deluxe box set sold out almost immediately and now crops up occasionally on eBay, usually at starting prices well over £200. The CD and vinyl versions are still more readily available, at the time of writing.

More to my surprise, the occasion was marked by the BBC deciding to reshow the film. This was a handy bonus, as our original agreement had expired in October 2018, so they had to negotiate a further payment to put it on again. I had to re-licence some of the film clips, but there was still a bit left over to put in the pot.

Search 4AD.com   SEARCH

Gene Clark: *4AD To Reissue Gene Clark's Masterpiece No Other This November*

10th September 2019

"One of the greatest albums ever made. Initially celebrated for its obscurity, No Other is now celebrated for its magnificence. It was in every way a magnum opus: epic, sprawling, poetic, choral, rococo."
The Guardian

4AD are thrilled to announce the reissue of Gene Clark's 1974 masterpiece *No Other* - one of the American singer-songwriter and Byrds founding member's finest works - coming out on November 8th 2019.

Available Across Four Formats: CD / Double CD / LP / Limited Edition Boxset
PRE-ORDER NOW FROM *GENECLARK.4AD.COM*

All pre-orders of the deluxe boxset from the 4AD store also include two flexi-discs of tracks not available anywhere else.

4AD announce the 'No Other' reissue.

AND IN THE END...

By the last months of 2019, once the 4AD reissue of 'No Other' was complete and the BBC's rescreening had been organised, the project was no longer taking over my life.

I was still looking after sales of the DVD, which by now were down to an average of less than ten a week; answering queries from fans and customers; and making sporadic attempts to find ways of extending the film's life through broadcasts or streaming. Apart from that, I've been able to move onto or return to other things – travelling just for pleasure and exploration, for example, now that's become possible again; making music with others who share at least some of my tastes; helping with grandchildren; and writing this book.

All of the efforts to find new outlets for the film have come to nothing, sadly, although we haven't completely given up trying. The big issue, as always, is the cost of licensing. Regardless of which channel is being used. And the fact that the streaming services, such as Netflix and Amazon Prime, don't accept individual submissions. They only take 'bundles' from studios or distributors. We've probably spoken with every credible distributor of documentaries, on both sides of the Atlantic, and we keep hitting the same sticking point, even when they seem very enthusiastic in the first instance. We would have made life much easier, if we'd followed the example of many other documentaries and included less music. But then we wouldn't have made the film we wanted to make.

The DVDs sold out in early 2021 and, as hoped, along with the BBC money, this had brought in enough to cover everything that had been spent on the various aspects of the project. Which was a great relief, as it confirmed the optimistic assurances I'd been giving Tricia for the past ten years, about refilling the hole in our pension fund.

We still get occasional requests for copies, via email or the Facebook page, so we could undoubtedly have sold more. But not enough to justify the cost of relicensing all the musical and archival content, as well as paying the higher unit cost of a more limited print run. All we can do is advise the enquirers to keep an eye on Amazon Marketplace and eBay, where second hand copies crop up every so often.

It's possible that there might be an unexpected surge in interest about Gene Clark, at some point, if one of his songs is given a new lease of life. It happened with Nick Drake, after his song 'Pink Moon' was used in a Volkswagen advert. It happened with Eva Cassidy, when Radio 2 started playing her music some years after her death. And it's happening with Kate Bush as I write this, following the use of 'Running Up That Hill' in the blockbuster TV series 'Stranger Things'.

If something similar happens, to bring Gene back into the spotlight, I've no doubt we'll get approaches about the film. We may even consider ways of rereleasing it ourselves. But I'm not holding my breath.

And if that is the end of the road – if the DVD becomes a collector's item and the film remains seen by only a select few (though not so few in the UK, thanks to the BBC) – I have no regrets. We're proud of what we achieved. We had a life enhancing experience doing it. We're delighted with the response we've had, from fans, critics and, most importantly, from Gene's family and friends. Perhaps best of all, it's enabled me to renew old friendships and make new ones, and to create some indelible memories with two of my sons. I may have devoted countless hours to it, for absolutely no financial return, but I'm richer in ways that don't appear on a bank statement.

I thoroughly recommend it.

Big thanks to everyone who's been helpful and supportive along the way, but especially: The Kendall family, the Clark family, Barry Ballard, Mark Cooper, Saul Davis, John Delgatto, Pattie DeMatteo, Henry Diltz, John Einarson, Cristina Fernández Via, Steve Fjelsted, Pete Frame, Chris France, Sid Griffin, Johnny Halliday (not the French Elvis!), Trace Harrill, Catherine Henry Rohlf, Scott Johnson, Jamie Johnston, Mike Kerry & Chris Hall – Start Productions, Andy Mawson, Stephania Minici, Ingrid Neimanis-McNamara, Whin Oppice, Domenic Priore, Johnny Rogan RIP, Jeff Rosen, Tom Slocum, Paul Surratt RIP, Dan Torchia, Rich Walker, Steve Webbon, Nick Wilson

Printed in Great Britain
by Amazon